Remember the days of old;
consider the generations long past.
Ask your father and he will tell you,
your elders, and they will explain to you.

—Deuteronomy 32:7 (NIV)

WHISTLE STOP Café = MYSTERIES =

RUMORS *are* FLYING

JEANETTE HANSCOME

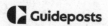

Whistle Stop Café Mysteries is a trademark of Guideposts.

Published by Guideposts
100 Reserve Road, Suite E200
Danbury, CT 06810
Guideposts.org

Scripture references are from the following sources: *The Holy Bible, King James Version* (KJV). *The Holy Bible, New International Version* (NIV). Copyright © 1973, 1978, 1984, 2011 by Biblica, Inc. Used by permission of Zondervan. All rights reserved worldwide. www.zondervan.com.

Cover and interior design by Müllerhaus
Cover illustration by Greg Copeland at Illustration Online LLC.
Typeset by Aptara, Inc.

ISBN 978-1-961126-90-9 (hardcover)
ISBN 978-1-961126-91-6 (epub)

Printed and bound in the United States of America
10 9 8 7 6 5 4 3 2 1

RUMORS are FLYING

CHAPTER ONE

Janet Shaw tied a brand-new red-and-white checked apron over her I'M A WHISK-TAKER T-shirt. She checked the bakery case to make sure she hadn't neglected any of the Whistle Stop Café's most popular offerings, though she'd added some fun fall goodies to lure people in on this first Monday after Labor Day. With school in full swing and the tourist season officially over, it felt like the perfect time to introduce autumn flavors like pumpkin and cranberry. Today, the featured treat was decadent pumpkin mini muffins with chocolate chips.

Her best friend and business partner, Debbie Albright, finished writing the breakfast and lunch specials on the chalkboard behind the counter then inhaled deeply. "Those muffins smell like heaven."

Janet admired the bakery tray she'd slid into the case, with its neat rows of puffy pumpkin goodness speckled with semisweet chocolate. "They really do, if I do say so myself. The first time I heard about pumpkin baked goods with chocolate chips, I thought it sounded strange. But now it's one of my favorite combinations. The flavors complement each other so well."

Debbie drew a little flourish under her list of specials.

Breakfast: Denver omelet with home fries or fruit
Lunch: BLT with avocado and choice
of fries, side salad, or soup
Soup of the day: Hearty vegetable

Debbie opened her apron pocket and dropped the chalk into it. "There we go. My attempt at creative lettering isn't quite as impressive as those muffins of yours. But it'll do for now."

"To be completely honest, I'm trying these muffins out on the customers before facing a much more brutal audience tomorrow."

"That's right. You start your workshop at the middle school tomorrow, you brave soul."

"Oh, it won't be that bad," Janet said, though she wasn't sure if she was trying to convince her friend or herself. "If the kids get too rambunctious, Julian will protect me. Besides, the Culinary Arts Club teacher, Miranda Sloan, will be there."

Julian Connor—the teenage son of Debbie's boyfriend, Greg—had been the one to recommend that Janet teach a workshop to kickstart the new school year for the Culinary Arts Club. As Miranda had explained to Janet, the club usually met once a week, but for the special September workshop, Janet would teach on Tuesday, Wednesday, and Thursday for the first week, and pop in for the regular Thursday afternoon meeting the next week to see how the kids applied what they learned.

Debbie strolled to the café entrance and unlocked the door. "Maybe you'll discover a baking prodigy."

"Wouldn't that be cool?" She'd already been dreaming of the possibility. "Inspiring the next generation of bakers is an exciting prospect. Although, right now, I'll be happy to make it through next week without making anyone cry, having to break up a fight, or dealing with a roomful of eye rolls because my recipes are totally lame."

"I don't think kids say 'totally lame' anymore."

"Well, the equivalent of it then."

"You'll be great." Debbie flipped the Open sign.

Janet busied herself with early morning customers stopping in for lattes, pastries, or a quick breakfast before work. Half an hour after the café opened, Harry Franklin walked in with his dog, Crosby, at his side like always. Behind them, a dark-haired young man pushed Ray Zink's wheelchair.

Harry held the door open. "Look who's joining me for breakfast this morning."

Ray pointed over his shoulder. "Jake here recently joined the staff at Good Shepherd and offered limo service this morning."

Debbie grabbed menus from the slot near the cash register. "Good morning, gentlemen. Nice to meet you, Jake." She escorted them to a table near the counter where they could chat with her and Janet and any other locals who happened to stop in.

Janet went over to hug her friends. "Look at you Ray, out on the town like you're nineteen again."

Ray gave Janet a smile that revealed a bit of the nineteen-year-old who still lived inside the ninety-eight-year-old veteran. "When Harry invited me to breakfast, I couldn't resist."

Janet leaned down to pet Crosby. "Good to see you too, boy."

Jake parked Ray's wheelchair at the table. "Enjoy your breakfast, Ray. Call when you're ready to be picked up. No rush."

"Will do. Thanks, Jake."

Jake gave Crosby a pat on the head before heading out. The dog curled up at Harry's feet.

"Or maybe, after some of Janet's delicious, nutritious food, Ray will be cured and can drive himself home," Harry said.

Ray pumped his fists in the air. "Janet's miracle breakfast."

"You guys are too much." Janet started making her way to the bakery case to find something to send home with Ray and Harry as a treat for later.

Debbie set a menu and a coffee mug in front of each of them just as Greg Connor came in. Her whole face lit up. "Well, good morning, stranger."

Greg greeted her with a hug and a peck on the cheek. "Good morning, beautiful. Hello, Janet."

"Hello there, Greg." Harry patted the empty chair beside his. "Want to join Ray and me for breakfast?"

"Thanks for the offer, Harry, but I better get my coffee and run. I'm meeting with the inspector on a house-flipping project I've finished in Uhrichsville. Can I take a rain check, though?"

"Of course you can."

While setting aside half a dozen mini pumpkin-chocolate chip muffins for Ray and Harry, Janet noticed the smile that had spread across Debbie's face and stuck after Greg called her beautiful. It was so nice to see Debbie finally giving in to her feelings for the handsome, good-hearted single dad. Janet had realized a long time ago that they were made for each other.

Janet took a large to-go cup off the stack for Greg. "What kind of coffee can I make for you, Greg?"

"Just a drip coffee with cream, and I think I'll take three of those pumpkin muffins with the chocolate chips as well. They smell amazing."

"Good choice."

Debbie took their orders and set it on the counter for Janet. "They made it easy for you. Two orders of pancakes with bacon and eggs over medium." Her eyes quickly shifted back to Greg. "How was the chamber of commerce meeting the other night? As fun-filled as always?"

Janet chuckled. A chamber of commerce meeting sounded about as fun-filled as a root canal. But it was one of Greg's passions, and with him excited about serving Dennison in that way, the group got a lot accomplished.

Greg took out his wallet. "Actually, it wasn't as boring as you might think. Christine Murray from the Dennison Preservation Society was there to propose a plan to buy that old Victorian home where Vera's Nursery used to be."

Janet filled Greg's cup with coffee. "I miss Vera's Nursery. Back when it was open, she had the best selection of flowers and plants in Dennison and Uhrichsville combined."

Since Vera retired and closed the store years ago, the 120-year-old house had fallen into disrepair. Over the summer, Janet had also read the sad news that Vera passed away.

She was glad to hear that the preservation society wanted to put the old house to good use. Memories of the house filled her mind like the scent of coffee filled the café. According to the stories she heard from her mother, the house had belonged to the Townsend family until 1945, when Jonas Townsend was reported killed in action.

When Janet was growing up, the house had been the Center Stage Academy of Voice and Dance. Janet had often sneaked into the backyard with her dolls and pretended she lived there. She'd watched dance classes through the windows, taught by the fairylike Miss Olivia with her perfect posture and graceful movements. She'd heard voice lessons given by Randolf Carson, opera singer by night, voice teacher by day.

In Janet's mother's day, it had housed a small private school that outgrew the building and made way for an art studio. But the Townsend house was most famous for its history as a boarding-house for soldiers returning from World War II, who either didn't have family or needed a place to recuperate from their time overseas and figure out their next step.

Janet handed Greg his cup of coffee and set the bag of muffins on the counter in front of him.

Debbie popped an extra muffin into the bag. "So, Vera's son and daughter-in-law didn't inherit the place after she passed?"

"Vera didn't actually own it. She rented it from the Grayson family, who bought it after Jonas Townsend was killed. Chad Grayson and his wife, Theresa, inherited it from Chad's father. But they think it's become a money pit and want to sell. I can't blame them. His dad could never afford to keep up with repairs after it was left to him, and the place has been renovated so many times it'll need a complete makeover. Other than the plumbing and roof repairs, I don't think it's been updated since the 1970s. The Dennison Preservation Society wants to buy it and turn it into a museum."

Janet brought her attention back to Harry and Ray. She picked up the order slip. "I'll get right on this."

Ray stroked Crosby's head. "No rush."

Harry added cream to his coffee. "We have all day to hang out here and make a nuisance of ourselves."

"Thanks, Harry. I really want to hear more about what the preservation society has planned." Janet put the order in her pocket and relaxed against the counter. "I'm curious why they want to turn it into a museum. We already have the depot museum right outside the café."

Greg took a couple of creamers out of one of the baskets on the counter. "This would be a lot different from the one here at the train station. They proposed an idea to create a place called the Dennison House. It will present the typical 1940s home, celebrate the house's years as a boardinghouse for soldiers returning from World War II, and be open for tours, field trips, and special events. Ladies' teas, that sort of thing."

"I think that sounds wonderful. So many of those old Victorian houses go up for sale, only to have the buyers gut them and update everything until they're no longer authentic and lose their historical charm."

"That's the exact point Christine brought up. The preservation society wants to restore the house to its former glory. There was even talk of making it part of the Christmas Train experience. They mentioned some fundraising events for the renovation that sound like a lot of fun."

Janet reached for the coffee carafe. If Harry and Ray were being so patient, the least she could do was offer them a warm-up. "So the chamber of commerce approved the plan?"

"We approved the idea of creating the Dennison House, but the Dennison Preservation Society will have to put in a bid for the house like anyone else would. We explained to Christine that we didn't have the authority to tell the Graysons who to sell their house to. The house needs a thorough inspection, and I'm sure it will also need extensive repairs, including a new roof, so the society has time to consider a budget and maybe even apply for some grants."

Debbie pulled a couple napkins from the nearest dispenser and put them in Greg's bag. "I bet the Graysons will like the idea of selling to a group like the Dennison Preservation Society. It'll give the house a purpose. They'll get to see it make a difference in the community."

"I sure hope so. As one who is constantly buying and selling houses, I know it might be tricky selling to a community group that's basically a nonprofit. But if they get as excited about the idea of the Dennison House as everyone was last night, the preservation society should be a shoo-in when the time comes to sell."

Janet handed Greg his bag. "It would be sad to see someone outbid them when they already have a plan for the house."

Greg paid. "I don't see this turning into a huge bidding war. As I mentioned, the house needs quite a bit of work. Personally, I think a museum is the perfect use for the place."

Janet took Ray and Harry's order out of her pocket. "So it's okay to start getting excited about the idea of a new tourist draw?"

"Cautiously excited, sure." Greg held up his cup as if in a toast. "I better be off." He gave Debbie a hug and a peck on the cheek that made her blush. "See you later."

She smiled. "See ya." After Greg left, Debbie faced Janet. "Well, that's exciting news."

"It is very exciting. Almost as exciting as me finally getting Harry's and Ray's breakfast started. It'll be right out, guys." Janet took their order to the kitchen.

She cracked four eggs onto the griddle and made the pancakes extra-large, musing all the while. A 1940s-style house would be a great draw. And if the Dennison Preservation Society did find a way to add it to the Christmas Train experience, it could breathe new life into a beloved tradition.

When Janet brought out the order, the pace in the café had started to pick up. She offered some fresh blueberries to her friends as an extra topping. "So, what do you two think of Greg's news about the Townsend house?"

Ray drizzled syrup over his pancakes. "I think it's a fine idea. Jonas would be pleased to have his home turned into a museum."

"Ray and Jonas were good friends," Harry told Janet.

Ray popped a bite of egg into his mouth. "Yep, we were friends from the time we sat next to each other in the first grade. We had our first trip to the corner together for clowning around during spelling. Twelve years later, we enlisted in the army a day apart. Sadly, he was one of the friends who didn't come home."

Janet wished for time to freeze so she could join Ray at the table for a while and hear about his old friend Jonas. Until that moment, Jonas's name had been one more detail of the history of an old house. Now, he was Ray Zink's childhood friend. "I'm sorry you lost such a good friend, Ray."

"I haven't thought about him in a long time. The whole story behind how the Townsend house went up for sale was tragic." Ray set his fork down. "Before we enlisted, Jonas was going out with a sweet girl named Gracie Pike. Everyone knew they would marry one day. A few months after he left for basic training, Jonas's parents were killed in an accident. Then Jonas was killed in war. The house went up for auction in late 1945. The couple who bought it opened it to soldiers who needed a place to stay a year later. But to me, it never stopped being Jonas's house." Ray picked up his fork again, but instead of scooping up another bite, he let it hover while his eyes drifted to nothing in particular.

Before Janet could ask if he was okay, a group of women bustled in for breakfast, sending Janet back to the kitchen to whisk eggs into omelets, fry sausage, and line the griddle with rows of pancakes. Her excitement over the idea of adding a place like the Dennison House to her hometown's historic offerings was edged out by the distant look she'd seen in Ray's eyes. This wasn't the first time she'd heard him talk about friends who had died in the war, but she sensed something different when Ray shared about Jonas. What was it?

Seeing Jonas's house put to use might be good for Ray. Janet edged her spatula under a golden pancake and flipped it neatly. She pictured Ray and Harry being some of the first to tour the Dennison House. They could offer suggestions for how to make the house authentic according to their own memories, especially with seasonal decorations.

She stacked three perfectly round pancakes on a plate. Maybe she could talk to the preservation society about dedicating the Dennison House to Jonas Townsend for his sacrifice. That would mean a lot to Ray.

As the breakfast rush tapered off, Janet took advantage of the slower place to leave the heat of the kitchen and catch up with the locals who lingered in the café. She found Ray and Harry still at their table while Crosby tracked Debbie's every move from his spot beside Harry's chair. He was rewarded when she dropped a bit of toast on the floor in front of him.

"You spoil him, Debbie," Harry told her, but there was no censure in his tone.

"No, I teach him to expect the same treatment here that I know he gets at home," Debbie replied with a grin. "I'm still thinking about the Townsend house. I've seen pictures of the place from the forties. If the preservation society can make the Dennison House happen and Christine is in charge, she'll turn it into something incredible. Especially at Christmas."

Janet went over to Harry and Ray's table and pulled out one of their extra chairs. "She could design it to be like Santa's Workshop." She put one hand on Ray's shoulder and the other on Harry's. "We have two elves right here."

Harry smacked the table. "I'm in."

The melancholy Janet had seen in Ray's eyes when talking about Jonas was nowhere in sight now. "They can turn my wheelchair into Santa's sleigh."

Debbie set a stack of dishes in the bin behind the counter. "Too bad it isn't in a spot where passengers could see the house from the train windows. But they can still see it on the way to the station."

"I know it's a bit premature to start making plans for the place," Janet admitted. "It's not a done deal yet. But I'm too excited. If it works out, it's going to be incredible."

"It is," Debbie agreed. She nodded toward the café entrance. "Do you want to finish cleaning this table, or do you want to take their order?"

A middle-aged couple stood patiently beside the counter.

Janet got her head back into the game of serving customers. "Welcome. Will this be for here or to go?"

"We'd like to eat here," the man replied.

"Glad to hear it. Feel free to have a seat anywhere you like and we'll be right with you," Janet assured them.

The tall, ponytailed woman thanked Janet as the couple made their way to a table against the wall lined with framed World War II prints.

Debbie went over with two menus. Janet went behind the counter in case they wanted something sweet. "Are you new to Dennison or just visiting?"

"Visiting." The man took a menu.

The woman took the other and laid it in front of her on the table. "We're staying in one of the Pullmans for a few nights."

Janet took two glasses out of the rack behind her and filled them with water. "You're smart to take a vacation after school starts. The Pullmans were booked all summer long." She carried the water to them. "Where are you from?"

The woman drew her glass closer. "Lakewood. Our youngest daughter just started college at Case Western Reserve, so we're officially empty nesters now."

Janet savored the moment of familiarity. "My daughter is in her second year at Case Western. It's a great school. If you give me your daughter's name before you leave, I'll pass it on to Tiffany in case they cross paths."

The man nudged his wife. "See, Chloe will be fine."

The woman's eye grew a little teary. "She will. I know." She blinked hard and took a deep breath. "Thank you."

"My name's Janet." She gestured to her co-owner. "And that's Debbie. If you're staying in a Pullman, you'll probably be here often. We might as well know one another's names."

Harry waved across the café. "I'm Harry Franklin, and this is Crosby. You'll definitely see us again."

Ray raised his hand. "Ray Zink. Why don't you join us?"

"That sounds lovely. I'm Laney Farrell." Laney went over and shook Harry's hand and Ray's then took one of the free chairs at the table.

Her husband followed. "And I'm Brian."

Debbie set out fresh utensils for them. "What inspired you to choose Dennison for your first trip as empty nesters? Not to put down our fine town or anything. I mean, we do have plenty of historic sites, and now is a great time to see them without having to fight the crowds. Our tourist season is about over."

Laney set her oversize tote bag on the floor. "Actually, we have a really big trip planned for October."

"Italy," Brian added.

"Good choice," Debbie said. "If I ever have a honeymoon, I want to go to Italy."

Janet made a mental note to pass that on to Greg. *I have a feeling that honeymoon is in your future.*

Laney picked up her menu. "This trip is more about checking out a house we're hoping to purchase for a B and B."

The idea of having a new bed and breakfast in Dennison as well as the preservation society's museum sent a fresh wave of excitement through Janet. She pictured summer tourists keeping both hopping from Memorial Day to Labor Day.

Debbie cleared an empty plate from the table behind Laney. "Would you like some coffee or tea while you look over the menu?"

Laney pulled a blue spiral notebook out of her tote bag. "Coffee sounds great."

Brian opened his menu. "Make that two, please."

Debbie headed toward the counter. "I'll make a fresh pot."

Janet noticed an empty basket of creamers and took it to the kitchen to replenish the selection. When she returned, the couple had moved their menus to the edge of the table to make room for the spiral notebook. Laney turned to a page that had a photo of an old house paper-clipped to the top.

"Are you ready to order?" Janet scooped up the menus and placed the basket in their place.

"I know it's not quite lunchtime, but a BLT sounds good," Laney said.

Debbie came over with the coffeepot and two mugs. "I consider a BLT the best of breakfast and lunch combined. Bacon and toast are breakfast foods, while the veggies are lunch foods." She took an order pad and pen out of her apron pocket.

Janet's gaze snagged on the picture in Laney's notebook. The house looked familiar.

Brian ordered a ham-and-egg scramble. Debbie jotted it down, tore off the order page, and handed it to Janet.

Laney moved the notebook aside and reached for the creamer basket. Janet sneaked another glance at the picture, now enhanced by midmorning sun. She froze at the sight of a large oak tree in front of the house, and a white painted gate leading to the backyard that was almost as familiar as the one where she'd grown up.

She folded Laney and Brian's order in half to keep her hands busy, so she wouldn't reach for the notebook and ask why they had a picture of the old Townsend house.

CHAPTER TWO

Dennison, Ohio
June 21, 1943

"Please don't cry, Gracie." Jonas Townsend wrapped a comforting arm around his girlfriend as they sat together on the park bench. "We both knew this day would come eventually."

As soon as he turned eighteen. That was what he and his friend Ray Zink had decided when America officially entered the war on December 8, 1941. They would enlist instead of waiting to be drafted. That way, they could choose whether to enter the army or the navy. He'd put off his trip to the recruitment office for a week after his birthday to give his mom and dad time to adjust to the idea. But today, he'd done it.

Gracie opened her handbag and pulled out a white handkerchief, dabbing at tears that kept coming.

"I know. It's right for you to go. All the men are enlisting. It's just..." Gracie's voice trembled and her lips quivered. "My brother is in France. My sister's husband is in the Pacific. My father is home because an injury that he got during the Great War exempts him now. I don't want anything to happen to you."

Jonas rubbed Gracie's shoulder. "I'll come back. I promise."

"You can't promise that. Last week, two boys from our high school were reported killed in action. Men are dying every day."

Jonas loosened his hold on Gracie's shoulder and slumped against the back of the bench. Every week, the Gazette listed the names. And all too often, those names were familiar. "You're right, Gracie. I can't promise that." What could he promise? He needed to do something to make her feel better. He couldn't stand to see her cry. "But I do promise to write as often as I can. I will stay true to you for as long as I'm away. And after all this is over, we'll get married."

She sniffed and wiped the rest of her tears. "Are you proposing?"

"Unofficially. I don't have a ring for you right now. Once I do, I'll propose correctly—with flowers and me on one knee. The whole bit."

Gracie made one more swipe across her cheeks. "As far as I'm concerned, you are my future husband. I promise to wait for you."

Jonas squeezed Gracie's hand and touched his forehead to hers. "Tell you what. I'll bring you back a present. Something pretty. Maybe I'll even find your engagement ring in Europe."

Gracie's smile lit up her lovely face and blue eyes. "You sound like you're going on vacation instead of off to war."

Jonas's stomach did a little flip. His promises did sound like they were coming from a guy who was going on an exotic trip. Like he would be gone for two weeks instead of who knew how long. Sitting there with Gracie, knowing how soon they would have to say goodbye, a little pretending felt rather nice. "Pretend I'm going on vacation then. Maybe that'll make it easier for you."

She leaned back, her eyes still shimmering with leftover tears. "You're right. I'll tell myself you're going to Paris with a French club. I heard some of the fancy private schools take trips like that. So let's say you go to one of those schools. It's a graduation gift from your folks. And I'm sick with envy." She gave him a playful punch on the arm, so light that Jonas barely felt it. "Oh, Jonas, how could you go without me? I've always longed to go to Paris."

"*There you go.*" *Jonas decided not to ruin the moment by reminding her that he'd barely scraped by with a B minus in his last year of French, so his parents probably wouldn't have sprung for a trip to Paris even if they could afford such a luxury. "Do you feel better?"*

"*I would feel better if you didn't have to go at all. But since you do, yes, I feel better than I did a minute ago.*"

"*I'm glad. Because it's late, and I better get you home. I don't want to leave you still upset.*"

She let out a sigh. "Thank you for caring so much about my feelings."

"*Of course I care. I love you, Gracie.*"

"*I love you too, Jonas.*"

Jonas pulled Gracie closer and gave her a tender kiss. "Before we know it, the war will be over, and then we can get married and start our life together."

He would give her a good life. One with the security he'd never had.

Jonas could still smell the verbena perfume that one of Gracie's aunts had given her for graduation when he bounded up the steps of the Victorian house that had been

in his family since the turn of the century. He'd been born here, and someday it would belong to him and Gracie. Their kids would probably be born in the hospital, but he would still bring them home to this house. He let the thought of a future with the girl he loved crowd out the dread of his much nearer and more uncertain future as a soldier.

He took off his jacket and hung it on the hall tree beside the door. "I'm home."

He waited for his mom or dad to respond. Mom would want to know how Gracie was doing with the news of his enlistment. Dad would be more concerned about him getting everything in order for basic training. Not that his father didn't care about Gracie. But these days, he seemed preoccupied and only asked about the basics.

"It's this war," Mom said whenever Jonas asked why Dad wasn't acting like himself.

Jonas never said it out loud, but he knew his father's mood more likely had to do with another business idea that hadn't worked out.

He walked into the living room. "Mom?"

The room was empty, the lights off, so he poked his head into the kitchen, expecting to see his parents talking at the table over cups of Postum. But the kitchen was as deserted as the living room.

How strange. *He'd seen Dad's Ford in the drive-way.* Maybe they went for a walk. *It was a nice night.*

Jonas shut off the kitchen light and made his way to the stairs. The sound of his father's voice in the study stopped him before his hand touched the banister. He started toward the study to say hello, but when he reached the door and found it slightly ajar, he caught a glimpse of his father talking on the phone.

Dad's voice sounded strained. "I know what I agreed to, but I can't get that kind of money so quickly." *He lowered his head and raked his hand through his graying sandy-brown hair.* "I just need a little more time. If you'd let me work out a payment plan—"

Jonas took a quick step to the side to avoid being seen while still being able to overhear his father's half of the tense conversation.

"If I'd known what this would turn into, I never would have participated in the first place."

The silence that came after that made the air feel thick and heavy.

"Listen, keep them out of this, okay? I'm the one who got into this mess."

Jonas's stomach lurched. Who was them? *Mom? Him?*

"Yes, I understand. You've made yourself very clear." *The phone receiver slammed against the cradle.*

Jonas hurried upstairs, careful to keep his steps as light as possible before his dad caught on to his eavesdropping. In the quiet of his bedroom, Jonas tried to make sense of what he'd overheard. What kind of mess had his dad gotten into? Every business he tried seemed to end with more money lost. Jonas had overheard enough heated conversations between his parents to know that managing finances wasn't his dad's forte.

He had sensed for a long time that he would be considered one of those kids from "the wrong side of the tracks," as people put it, if not for Dad inheriting his parents' house. His dad was a kind, God-fearing man, but some of his habits were becoming Jonas's motivation to go to college after the war ended and get a degree that would make it possible for him to support Gracie without her having to worry about him draining funds on shady ventures.

His suitcase stood in the corner, waiting for him to pack the essentials for basic training. As he started changing into his pajamas, he felt as if he might be leaving one war for another.

The door to his parents' bedroom at the end of the hall slammed shut, making the wall shake. He tried to ignore the heated exchange that came next. Then his mother started crying, and he couldn't tune it out anymore.

"Larry, I told you he couldn't be trusted."

"It was just a card game."

"Just *a card game? How can you say that? We could lose everything because of this.*"

Jonas sank onto the foot of his bed. Dad, what did you do?

CHAPTER THREE

*J*anet couldn't take her eyes off the faded black-and-white photo clipped to the college-ruled page. According to Eileen Palmer, when Larry, Bridget, and Jonas Townsend lived in the house, they'd painted it a cheery robin's-egg blue with white trim. The couple who bought it after the Townsends died had kept the color the same for its cheerfulness, insisting that the veterans would benefit.

Now the house was gray with cracking red trim, but the giant oak tree in the yard that had always distinguished it from other houses on the block stood out in the photo as much as it had when Janet was a child.

"Janet?" Laney asked, drawing Janet's attention back to the present. "Is everything okay?"

Janet ran her hands over the front of her apron. "Yes. I'm sorry to be nosy, but where did you get that picture?"

Laney tapped her spoon on the side of her mug then set it on a napkin. "I found it in that notebook. Isn't the house adorable?"

Janet nodded. "It is."

Debbie came to Janet's side. Her friend's small gasp told Janet that she also recognized the house.

Laney moved the notebook to her place mat. "It's been our dream for years to open our own B and B. We have something kind of quirky in mind—vintage-style theme rooms that reflect periods of history. Regency, roaring twenties, the forties. So of course the house needs to be historic as well."

"That sounds wonderful," Debbie said.

It did sound wonderful. A perfect complement to the Dennison House. If only the preservation society and the Farrells didn't have the same house in mind.

Laney ran her fingers along the edges of the photo. "My grandfather died of a heart attack about a month ago, at ninety-eight. Before he passed, I think he might have been trying to write his life story. This notebook is full of partial stories that have us baffled. He taped a key to the inside of the back cover without a clue of what it opens."

"How odd," Ray said.

Laney freed the snapshot from the paper clip and flipped it over. "We found the photo in Grandpa Abe's notebook. See that?" She pointed to a note on the back, printed in careful black letters. *For Laney and Brian.* "When I saw the photo, I thought the place would be perfect for our B and B."

"If it's even for sale," Brian pointed out.

"We know it's vacant, at least. I checked the address before we came," Laney said. "Anyway, we saw what Grandpa wrote on the back and thought about what Dennison is known for—this historic train station, the museum. And Grandpa Abe obviously wanted us to get this house if he wrote our names on the back." She rested her fingertip under another note at the bottom. *Home, Dennison, Ohio.* "I had no idea that Grandpa ever lived in Dennison. But if this house is for sale, we definitely want to check it out." Laney handed the photo to Janet.

The longer she studied the old Victorian house that Laney's Grandpa Abe had called *Home*, the harder Janet had to work to keep from blurting out, "This can't be your grandfather's home. The last member of the Townsend family was killed in action in 1945."

Unless Laney was related to Chad Grayson. No, that couldn't be right. If that were the case, Laney wouldn't need to wonder if the house was for sale.

Janet gave the picture back to Laney. "Are you sure your grandfather wrote the notes on the back?" She bit her lip, wishing she could take back the question. Laney and Brian had come in for breakfast and now probably felt interrogated by crazy locals.

"I'm positive." Laney held the spiral notebook out to Janet so she could see the neat printing. "The notes on the photo and Grandpa's entries in his book are in the same handwriting."

Janet read the writing on the lined page. *I left Dennison, Ohio, on June 28, 1943...* The handwriting was undeniably the same.

Laney carefully returned the photo to its place under the paper clip. "I must admit it confused me too. I asked my mom about the picture, and she'd never seen it before. Grandpa's name was Abe Halner, and he always told me he lived in St. Louis until 1950 when he moved to Cincinnati for a job. When my parents moved us all to Lakewood, Grandma and Grandpa Halner moved too. Not once did Grandpa Abe mention Dennison."

Janet noticed Ray and Harry listening with rapt attention. If Laney's grandfather had ever lived in Dennison, they would know. Harry was well-versed in Dennison history, and he and Ray knew everyone in town. When she reached her nineties, she hoped to be half as sharp and in tune with the community as they were.

Debbie began to move away, her brown eyes communicating the same confusion that Janet felt. But she kept it to herself, which was more than Janet was doing.

Janet stepped away from the table. "I'm sorry. I should get out of your business and make your food."

Laney returned her grandfather's notebook to her tote bag. "No need to apologize."

On her way to the kitchen, Janet overheard Laney and Brian chatting with Ray and Harry. When she returned with the Farrells' meals, Harry asked, "What did you say your grandfather's last name was?"

"Halner," Laney said. "Abe Halner."

Debbie went over with the coffeepot and refilled Ray's mug. "Ray, did you ever know an Abe Halner?"

Ray folded his arms and gazed at the ceiling for a moment. Finally, he said, "I never knew any Halners. Did you, Harry?"

Harry shook his head. "I knew some Halters, but not anyone named Halner. Do you mind if I have a closer look at your picture?"

"Not at all." Laney pulled the notebook back out of her tote, removed the photo, and handed it to Harry. "I'd be happy for any help."

"If anyone can figure out your grandfather's possible connection to Dennison, these two can," Janet told her.

Harry examined the photo. "This is the Townsend house, all right." He handed it to Ray.

"Oh, yeah, that's it for sure." Ray's gaze was glued to the photo. "Do you think your grandfather could have seen the picture online and printed it out for you, knowing you were interested in buying one for your bed and breakfast?"

"I wondered that too, until I saw *home* written at the bottom and his note mentioning Dennison," Laney said. "What I'm hoping is that the key he taped into the notebook will fit the house. It's not the size of your typical house key, but it's worth a shot if someone will let us try."

Brian took a swig of coffee. "Also, the picture doesn't look like a computer printout. It reminds me of pictures I used to see in my grandparents' photo album. It's possible that he printed it on photo paper, but it's not likely he would have gone to such trouble."

Janet thought over the details she'd seen in the photo. There was no question of its authenticity, unless Brian and Laney were experts at creating computer-generated images. The faded black-and-white image had the standard white border and glossy finish of pictures created from film.

"How do you know the house?" Laney asked.

Harry took a minute to fill the Farrells in on the house's history and Ray's friendship with Jonas.

Janet moved behind Ray and studied the picture over his shoulder. Even in black-and-white, the house was positively idyllic with its long porch and shutters and the grand oak tree.

Ray pointed to a bicycle that Janet had missed. "This picture was taken before Jonas left for the war. That's his bike leaning against the garage door. He saved all his paper route money to buy it. We were twelve at the time." He gave the picture back to Laney.

Laney stared at it. "How does my grandpa work into all this?"

Judging by everyone else's expressions, that was the question on all their minds.

While preparing for the lunch rush to begin, Janet tried to push away her disappointment over the rapid twist of events that had come with the Farrells' visit to the café.

She tore open a new package of cheddar cheese. "I guess we can say goodbye to the Dennison House."

"Not necessarily." Debbie set a fresh loaf of sourdough bread on the work counter. "No matter how Laney's grandfather got that picture, he didn't own the house when he passed away. The Grayson family did."

"True." Janet checked her watch. Ten o'clock. Paulette Connor—Greg's mother, who worked at the café part-time—was due to arrive any minute for the lunch shift. They needed to focus on their customers, not a house that wasn't even for sale yet. "But it might make things more challenging for the preservation society to buy the house if the Farrells put in a bid as well."

Debbie opened a jar of mayonnaise. "Ray was as confused by the photo as we were."

"I would be confused too if a complete stranger walked in with a picture of, say, my grandmother's house and said, 'Hey, check out what I found in my grandpa's stuff. I think it might be mine now.'" Janet heard the bell over the door jingle. "How in the world did

Laney's grandpa end up with a picture of Ray's childhood friend's home?"

Paulette hurried into the kitchen. "Hello, ladies. I'm ready for lunch duty." She took an apron. "Did Greg tell you about the preservation society wanting to buy the old Townsend house? What a fun addition that will be."

Janet took the lid off the pot of vegetable soup to stir it. "He sure did." *Should I tell her about the Farrells?* Maybe later, after the lunch crowd. "It'll be great if it works out."

But Debbie had other ideas. "Hey, Paulette, you've lived in Dennison for years. Have you ever heard of a family with the last name Halner?"

Paulette tied her apron. "No."

"And no one with that last name ever lived in the Townsend house?"

"Not unless they were a boarder after World War II."

Debbie touched Janet's arm. "I bet that's the connection." She told Paulette, "Don't worry, we'll fill you in later," and changed the topic to the lunch special.

Janet turned up the heat on the soup. An image of one of Abe Halner's notebook pages flashed through her mind. *No, that can't be it.* Abe wrote that he had left Dennison in 1943. The Townsend house hadn't opened for boarders until 1946, after the war ended.

Which meant they still had no answers.

CHAPTER FOUR

Dennison, Ohio
June 22, 1943

When Jonas saw his friend Ray Zink walk through the door of Milton's Ice Cream and Candy Shoppe, he instantly knew where he'd been before coming to celebrate his eighteenth birthday. The recruiting office. Jonas knew the expression by now, not to mention the folder under Ray's arm. Ray looked exactly like Jonas had felt the previous day—a head taller than when they'd accepted their high school diplomas mere weeks before, but still processing what he'd done.

Jonas pushed his glass of root beer and the heaviness in his heart aside. "Hey, Ray. Happy birthday."

"Thanks." Ray came over to the ice cream counter and perched on the stool beside Jonas's. "Yesterday,

I was an ordinary seventeen-year-old kid. Today, I'm an official adult."

Eighteen. Old enough to vote and old enough to join the fight in Europe, Africa, and Asia.

Ray put the folder with its United States Army insignia in his lap. "I'm all signed up. I leave for boot camp in three days."

Jonas reached for his root beer again. "I'm leaving on the same train. I enlisted yesterday as planned." The reality of what that meant triggered an instant knot in his stomach. We're going to war. He would leave having no idea what had led up to the phone call he overheard the night before, or his mother's tearful, "We could lose everything." Nor would he witness the outcome.

Would he have a home to return to after the war?

He didn't realize how quiet he'd gotten until Ray put his hand on his shoulder. "Are you okay?"

Jonas let his straw drop into the fizzy brown drink. "Sure, I'm okay. Can I buy you a soda to celebrate your big day? Your birthday and your service?"

"That would be nice. Thank you."

For old times' sake, Jonas pinched Ray's arm. "A pinch to grow an inch." He punched his shoulder. "And a sock to grow a block."

Ray laughed as he scanned the meager fountain menu that mostly featured the soda flavors available. Ice cream was one of the many treats limited by rationing. As Jonas waited for Ray to decide on a drink, it hit him that they would soon be in the group that luxuries like ice cream were saved for— the soldiers.

Mr. Milton came over to the counter. "What can I get for you, Ray?"

"I'll have a root beer, please."

Jonas reached into his pocket for a nickel. "It's on me, Mr. Milton."

Ray moved his recruitment folder to the counter. "But don't let me forget what I came in for—a pint of vanilla ice cream to go with the pie Mom is baking for my birthday. She told me a day like this calls for sacrificing some ration coupons."

Jonas knew he should say something in return, but no words came out. Mr. Milton saved him by delivering Ray's root beer and congratulating him on his birthday.

Then they were alone again, and Jonas went back to feeling torn between wanting to tell Ray what he had heard at home and keeping it to himself.

Two girls from their high school came in. They went straight to the penny candy jars at the end of the counter, close enough to hear him and Ray talking. Jonas had lived in a small town long enough to know when people listened in, they often talked. Besides, this was Ray's day. He didn't need Jonas's troubles.

Jonas raised his root beer glass. "To winning the war."

Ray clinked his glass against Jonas's. "Cheers."

Jonas lowered his drink and stirred it with his straw. "I can't believe we're really doing this."

"Me neither. I saw three other guys from our graduating class at the recruitment office today."

Jonas took a sip and let the sweetness linger on his tongue before saying, "I saw Mr. Carson." It had felt so surreal to see his gym teacher, who once ordered him to do twenty extra push-ups for being tardy, enlisting in the army.

Ray poked the foam at the top of his root beer with his straw. "How did Gracie take the news?"

"A lot of tears, but in the end, she promised to wait. She will too. She's a great girl."

For the next thirty minutes, they tried to talk as if they didn't have a trip to boot camp ahead of them, but reality kept making its way into the conversation. Jonas considered that all the more reason not to drag things down more by bringing up his personal worries.

"Thanks for the root beer, Jonas."

"You're welcome." Jonas put a tip on the counter. "I'll follow you out."

Ray handed over ration coupons for the ice cream then picked up his folder and waved goodbye to Mr. Milton.

"Happy birthday, Raymond."

"Thanks, Mr. Milton."

Outside, they walked down the street in companionable silence, pausing at the entrance to Dennison Station. There was a line of servicemen at the canteen, where the Salvation Army volunteers offered them sandwiches, coffee, and doughnuts to eat during their journey east.

"In a few days, we'll be boarding one of those trains." Ray's words came out sounding like they were coming from someone else.

"Yeah." Jonas turned away from the train station. The closer he got to home, the more he dreaded being there. That morning, he'd asked his dad what was wrong.

"Nothing you need to concern yourself with, Son. You have enough on your plate right now."

But it is my concern. Something's going on, and I want to know what it is. I need to know my parents will be okay.

"Is everything all right, Jonas? You're not acting like yourself today."

Jonas scuffed the toe of his shoe against the ground. "I don't want to spoil your birthday."

"Aw, come on." Ray stopped beside him. "I'm eighteen, not eight. I'm way past the stage of not wanting anything to spoil my birthday. Besides, I can tell something's eating at you, and it'll spoil my day more to keep wondering about it. Tell me what's on your mind."

"Okay, since you asked." Jonas glanced over his shoulder to check for prying ears from the neighborhood or church, anyone who might hear his family's woes and make them public knowledge. He plopped onto a nearby bench, keeping his voice low. "I'm worried about my folks. I think my dad might have gotten himself into trouble."

Ray set his bag on the bench. "What kind of trouble?"

"I'm not sure. Last night I heard him talking on the phone, and it sounded like he might owe someone money. Then I overheard him and Mom arguing. It was something about a card game, and Dad trusting someone who was bad news."

"A card game? Does your dad gamble?"

Until last night, Jonas would have said no at once. Betting on horses was legal in the state, but other forms of gambling weren't. "I know he plays poker sometimes. I've seen him play for matchsticks and pennies but never serious money." He'd heard his mother joke with friends that one benefit of being strapped for cash was that her husband didn't have extra to waste on card games. "But now I'm not so sure."

"Maybe it's not as bad as you think. If my dad lost so much as a dollar in a card game, my mom would have a fit. Every cent matters these days."

Jonas shook his head. "This was about more than a dollar. Mom was crying. I heard her tell Dad we could lose everything."

Ray rested his hand on Jonas's shoulder. "I'm really sorry, Jonas."

"This morning, my mom's eyes were red and puffy. I asked why she'd been crying, and she said everything was fine. That she had hay fever."

"Moms like to protect their kids from bad news."

Jonas got up from the bench. "I'm getting ready to head off to war. I think I can handle the truth about what's going on." He managed a small smile for Ray, who was clearly willing to keep listening even though he had a bag of melting ice cream. "Thanks for letting me talk."

"Anytime." When they reached the corner where they'd parted ways during countless walks home from school, Ray put his bag on the ground and held out his hand. Jonas put his on top of Ray's, and they alternated until one of them couldn't reach any higher. It had been their version of a secret handshake since they were eight years old. "Man. You beat me again," Ray said as he picked up his ice cream.

Jonas elbowed him. "I was going to let you win since it's your birthday, but I decided that wouldn't be right. They won't let you win in boot camp."

"I can see you're feeling better."

"A little." It always helped to talk to Ray.

"Try not to worry. Your dad has gotten into scrapes before, and they always ended up okay."

Okay until the next one.

Jonas rounded the corner and headed toward the blue Victorian that he would soon say goodbye to. He called back over his shoulder to Ray. "This is one of those times when I hope I'm making a big deal about nothing."

CHAPTER FIVE

On Tuesday morning, Janet hoped Laney and Brian would come into the café with an update on Abe Halner's connection to the Townsend house. Instead, the café was busy with locals who'd heard about the Dennison Preservation Society's plan to buy the house. If the Farrells came in after the lunch rush, Janet missed it. She'd had to go home at one to make final preparations for the Culinary Arts Club presentation.

At 3:05 p.m., she pulled into the Dennison Middle School parking lot and spotted Julian beside the flagpole, where he had insisted on meeting her. He trotted to her car as Janet pulled out her bag filled with canned pumpkin, chocolate chips, spices, and muffin cup liners.

"Hello, Julian."

"Hi, Janet. Let me get this for you." He took the bag from her.

"Why thank you, kind sir." Janet checked her purse to make sure she hadn't forgotten the copies of her muffin recipe. "You didn't have to meet me. I know my way around. Though now that I'm here, I'm getting a terrible feeling that I'm in seventh grade again and forgot my locker combination."

Julian laughed. "I know, but they're finishing up a renovation of the quad, so we have to take a detour." He led her around the taped-off quad.

Janet stopped to take in the updates. In her day, the quad had been an open area with a circular mound of grass, surrounded by concrete seating. Tiffany's generation had rocks and succulents in place of the grass. Now, the quad was downright inviting, with columns and an overhang to provide shade and picnic tables in place of the circular seating. "This is really nice. I need to take a picture later and send it to Tiffany."

"Yeah, it's coming out pretty good." Julian pushed open the entrance to the administration building. "Here's where you sign in, so if any of us kids come up missing, they know who to blame it on."

"Julian, are you scaring away our volunteers again?"

Janet immediately recognized the woman behind the administration desk. Allison Hutchins had worked in the office when Tiffany attended the middle school. "Hi, Allison. I'm here to do a baking workshop for Miranda Sloan."

Allison directed Janet to a fat binder with a sunflower-topped pen chained to it. "She told me to keep an eye out for you. My granddaughter is in the Culinary Arts Club, so I look forward to benefiting from her skills." She thumbed to the section marked *Volunteers*. "I'm sure you know the drill. It's the same as when you signed Tiffany out early, but a different page. Sign in here, and sign out when you leave. Our little comedian over there can escort you to the Culinary Arts room."

Janet picked up the pen and prepared to complete the sign-in sheet that, other than the pen topper, hadn't changed in six years. She held up the pen. "This is new."

Allison showed her another one with a feather that made the pen resemble a quill. "I could not look at that old pink pom-pom pen topper for one more day."

Janet did one more bag check. *Recipe, ingredients, apron without a goofy slogan in case the kids don't share my humor. All set.* "Okay, Julian. Take me to the Culinary Arts room."

Julian cocked his head to the left. "Right this way."

As she followed Julian down the long hall, passing girls and boys who were still waiting for their first big growth spurt, Janet's mind flooded with flashbacks to her awkward middle school years. Same hallway, different posters, new flooring. Baking was one of the activities that had helped her find her place in the often-cruel world of teen life. Winning the Outstanding Achievement Award in Foods II may not have been the coolest accomplishment in the history of what was then Dennison Junior High. But when Debbie didn't get asked to the dance, or one of their friends was cut from cheerleading tryouts, Janet knew how to make everything better. With brownies.

In the Culinary Arts room, fifteen seventh and eighth graders sat in groups of three or four around large worktables. Each station around the perimeter of the room had a stove, refrigerator, sink, and cupboards, and every girl with long hair had it bound into a ponytail or a messy bun. At some point in the past few decades, the school district had updated the appliances, so the stations no longer resembled a 1970s housewares catalog.

A young woman who looked like she had recently graduated from college came to shake Janet's hand. "Hi, I'm Miranda. Thank you so much for doing this. The kids are super excited."

"It's nice to finally meet you in person." Janet reached into her tote bag for her apron. "I'm excited to be here." She was thankful that she'd thought to change out of her BAKING IS MY HAPPY PLACE sweatshirt. These were some serious bakers.

Julian took one of many white aprons off a hook and joined a table with two girls and a boy with a mop of thick curls. "Be nice to her, guys. Janet—I mean, Mrs. Shaw—is a friend of mine."

Half the group smiled. The other half kept critical eyes on Janet.

"Thank you, Julian." Janet took her place up front. "I'm Janet Shaw, co-owner of the Whistle Stop Café." Even though she'd seen all the faces at least once and knew some of the kids from church, she broke the ice with, "How many of you have been to the café?"

Every hand went up.

"I thought I saw a lot of familiar faces in here."

Why do I feel like the biggest dork in the world right now? She glanced down at her tennis shoes. Not exactly the latest style. She shook herself. She wasn't there to make a fashion statement. She was there to pass on her knowledge and skills.

A girl with a long strawberry-blond ponytail took out a notebook and pen.

"Bethany," the girl beside her said, "this is a club. You don't have to take notes."

Bethany reacted with a firm, "Shh. I don't want to miss anything." She gave Janet her full attention.

Janet's stomach did a cartwheel under the pressure, but she squared her shoulders. "Let's start with our recipe. I thought we'd make something a little different. One of my personal fall favorites, pumpkin-chocolate chip muffins."

She overheard one boy whisper to his neighbor, "That's different?"

Janet ignored the comment. "For a little extra challenge, we're going to make mini muffins."

Within five minutes of her talk on the craft of muffin making, she could tell the kids were way beyond this level of baking.

"I know muffins seem very basic, but there's an art to them. For example, you don't want to overmix the batter. That will make your muffins tough instead of light and fluffy."

A girl at Julian's table rolled her eyes, and Bethany jotted down a note.

"And," Janet continued, "you need to be careful with baking time on mini muffins."

The eye roller at Julian's table raised her hand. "Because they're, like, smaller than regular muffins."

"That's enough, Anna," Miranda said.

Julian glared at Anna.

What was it about being in a middle-school classroom that made a woman feel thirteen again? "You know what? It sounds like you kids are ready to roll." She grabbed her stack of recipes and tried to separate the top sheet from the one under it, but suddenly she was all thumbs. She gave up and offered the stack to Bethany. "Would you like to pass these out for me?"

"Sure."

"My plan was to have you work in groups." Which she didn't need to say, since obviously there weren't enough ovens for them to work individually. "If you need help, let me know."

Over the next fifteen minutes, she watched the kids scoop, measure, sift, and stir. She went around to each group to offer assistance that none of them needed.

Julian held up a stack of the fall leaf-themed mini-muffin cup liners she'd brought. "These are cool, Mrs. Shaw."

"Thanks, Julian. Mini muffins don't have to have wrappers, but I thought those were fun." She wandered over to Miranda's desk. "These kids don't need me. They already know how to bake."

"In order to be in the club, students must have taken at least Culinary Arts I and earned a B or higher."

Janet hadn't realized that. "Then I'll need to come up with something more challenging for tomorrow."

The next morning, Janet poured out the whole humiliating story to Debbie and Patricia Franklin, Harry's granddaughter and local attorney. As one of their regulars, Patricia got to hear about a lot of Janet's baking adventures.

"Everyone's muffins came out looking like they belonged on a baking show. I had planned to teach them how to make their own pizza today, but they could probably teach me how to make it." Janet opened the bakery case and took out a piece of coffee cake for Patricia. "I need to come up with something much better than pizza or Anna the eye-roller will vote me out of the Culinary Arts Club."

Patricia took a napkin out of the dispenser on the counter. "I know this is kind of last minute, but how about teaching them to bake something that relates to one of their classes?"

Janet nodded. "That's why I talk out my problems with you. I knew you'd have something for me. What are students studying in eighth grade these days?"

Debbie set Patricia's iced peppermint mocha in front of her. "Over the weekend, I had dinner at Greg's. The boys were talking about their reading lists, comparing them with what Greg and I had to read in school. Julian mentioned that the eighth graders are reading *The Diary of Anne Frank* as part of a World War II unit. What if you challenged the kids to make recipes from World War II?"

"That might be fun." But what World War II recipe would impress such advanced young bakers?

Patricia patted her mouth with a napkin. "It isn't a recipe, but how about a lesson on food rationing?"

Debbie ran a damp cloth over the milk steamer. "I like that. You can tell the kids about the ration books that every family had for buying things like sugar and butter."

Janet considered how hard it was for her to limit sugar and fats in her baking. At one point when she'd worked at the Third Street Bakery, her boss, Charla Whipple, had wanted to add some low-sugar, low-fat options to their menu. They had a series of flops before they came up with something that tasted good. "That's a great idea. I can bring the amount of sugar and fats that the average family had per week and challenge them to bake with it."

"Lots of people had to do it, so we know it can be done," Patricia said. "But it'll also give them a chance to problem-solve."

Janet searched her brain for something she could pull together in time for that day's workshop. "Hopefully, as kids who love to bake, they'll appreciate how creative they would have had to be if they were thirteen years old in the forties."

Debbie put the cap back on the chocolate syrup. "If you really want to get them invested, make it a contest. The student with the most creative twist on a World War II-era baked treat could win a gift card or something."

Kids did like gift cards. Janet realized she'd left the bakery case open, and an idea struck as she closed it. She smiled at Debbie. "How about a gift card to a store that teenagers like *and* a chance to have their creation featured in the café as a special for the last week of September?"

Patricia pinched off a piece of her coffee cake. "Wow. If I could bake, I would enter that contest. You might even be able to ask a local business to donate the gift card."

Debbie leaned against the counter. "The winner will need to make something extra-special though. Something creative."

"Definitely." Janet grabbed an order pad and tore off the top page to jot down their ideas. "How about if we go a step further? The profits earned from the winner's culinary delight will go to the Culinary Arts Club."

The front door opened, and Harry walked in with Crosby at his heels.

Debbie went over to welcome him, and Janet started heading to the kitchen. "I'm excited now. This is going to be so fun."

Harry took a seat on the stool beside his granddaughter's. "What's going to be fun? What did I miss out on?"

Patricia gave her grandfather a quick hug. "Janet is going to introduce the Culinary Arts Club to the concept of butter and sugar rationing."

Harry wrinkled his nose. "That's kinda mean. I developed my sweet tooth because of sugar rationing."

Janet shared the whole story behind the rationing challenge.

"Okay, now I see why you think this will be fun. Now that you mention it, the opportunity to be creative might open their eyes in a good way. I learned to appreciate treats because they were so rare."

Janet reached for her notepad again. "What were some of your favorites? I'm trying to come up with something for this afternoon."

"My favorite was apple pandowdy. It's kind of like a cobbler— baked fruit sweetened with a little maple syrup or brown sugar and topped with strips of pie crust." Harry licked his lips. "It was so good."

Janet wrote down, *Apple pandowdy. Find recipe.*

"Turnovers were always a hit too. Mom used whatever fruit she had on hand."

"Now, those I can pull together today without a problem." She could take apples and some other options for the kids to choose from as well, like canned pears and frozen berries. "Thanks, Harry. You saved my afternoon."

After the noon rush, with Paulette busy in the kitchen, Janet made a list of items for the afternoon's rationing challenge. She put a jar of apple filling into the shopping bag.

"You know, Paulette, I don't think I ever stopped to think about how little sugar people lived on in the forties."

Paulette laid a grilled cheese sandwich on the grill. "I don't think I could do it."

"I think I would be the whiniest woman in town if I had to cut back on crucial baking supplies like butter and sugar. These families were tough." Janet took off her apron, folded it, and nestled it around the apples in the bag. She grabbed the handles and took a deep breath. "Well, off I go."

"Have fun this afternoon."

"It'll be interesting to see their responses to being restricted in this way."

Janet folded her list and slipped it into her sweatshirt pocket then went out to the bakery counter. She confirmed that Debbie and Paulette had plenty of cookies, muffins, and other goodies to get them through closing time then remembered something that might get the kids in the Culinary Arts Club a little more excited about her workshop.

"Hey, Debbie, do we have any of those coupons for free cookies left?"

"They're in the drawer under the cash register."

Janet found the stack and was stashing them in her tote bag when the café door opened, and Christine Murray, who worked on the Dennison Preservation Society, all but flew inside.

Like Debbie, Christine was a local who'd left Dennison, grown tired of fast-paced city life, and returned to her hometown. Janet had gone to high school with Christine, but they always ran in different circles, Janet with the cooking afficionados and Christine with the student counsel and debate team. Janet knew her just well enough to recognize that when the perfectly coiffed, impeccably dressed woman entered a room without a determined "Guess how I plan to turn Dennison around for the better today?" smile on her face, something had gone terribly wrong. Today, Christine wore her "Dennison has gone to the dogs" expression.

Before Janet could say hello, Christine dropped her high-end black purse on the counter and requested a latte with an extra espresso shot. She ran her hand over her dark shoulder-length hair and gazed longingly into the bakery case.

"Can I get you something sweet to go with your latte?" Janet offered.

"Oh, I shouldn't."

"Whether you should or shouldn't, you look like you could use a little pick-me-up."

Christine gave her a wry smile. "You've got that right. I'll have a peanut butter cookie."

"In a to-go bag, or for here?"

"I better take it to go."

Debbie got started on the latte, and Janet bagged the cookie. "Do you want to talk about it?" she asked. She had a feeling she knew what was wrong. Christine had most likely heard about the Farrells' interest in the Townsend house.

"If you really want to know, I am a bit upset right now."

Janet handed her the bag. "If it's not prying, do you want to talk about why?"

Christine plopped herself onto a stool. "Since you and Debbie know Greg Connor, I'm sure you heard about the preservation society's plan to buy the old Townsend house and turn it into a museum."

"Yes, we were so excited when we heard."

"I already talked to two major donors about grants for the remodeling process. I thought we were a shoo-in. Then I talked to Chad and Theresa Grayson, the couple that owns the house now, and they told me someone else is interested as well."

"Brian and Laney Farrell?"

"Yes. How did you know?"

Debbie poured steamed milk into Christine's cup. "They came into the café on Monday. They seem like nice people."

"I'm sure they are very nice people. But their interest might put an end to the preservation society's plan. They want to turn the house into a B and B. With theme rooms." Christine said *theme rooms* as if Brian and Laney planned to open a shady nightclub. "It makes me sick. Dennison could have a museum that honors a major era in our history, but instead, it could end up with a tacky themed B and B."

Janet glanced over at Debbie, whose expression reflected her own reaction. They'd both thought the B and B idea sounded kind of fun, even if it would squelch the Dennison House.

Debbie put a lid on Christine's coffee. "Don't give up yet, Christine. Like you, they'll have to wait for the house to officially go up for sale."

Christine took out her cookie and broke off a piece. "The worst part is, they claim to have a picture of the house with a note on it that says Mrs. Farrell's late grandfather wanted them to have it. Her grandfather never lived in Dennison. I did an internet search for his name." She popped the bite into her mouth. "I think she made the whole story up. They're scammers. I'm sure of it."

Janet pictured the friendly couple. They had seemed more like ordinary tourists excited to start the next phase of their lives than scammers.

Debbie flipped on the espresso maker. "Christine, isn't it a bit premature to assume the Farrells are scammers? What could they possibly have to gain? It's not as if they can expect to get the house for free, even if Laney's grandfather did live in it at one time, which he obviously didn't."

Christine dropped the rest of the cookie back into her bag. "They could gain favor with the Graysons, of course. Play on their emotions. I can already tell Chad and Theresa are falling for it. They're planning to meet with the Farrells tomorrow to give them a tour. There are Victorians up for sale all over Tuscarawas County, and the Farrells had to choose this house? Excuse me, *research* the house that Grandpa left in his mysterious notebook."

Janet handed Christine a napkin for her bag. It was tempting to remind Christine that her point about other houses in the area could also apply to the Dennison Preservation Society. She'd seen three lovely old houses for sale in Dennison and Uhrichsville in the past week. "Try not to jump to conclusions. The Farrells will have to put in an offer on the house like everyone else."

Debbie put a lid on Christine's cup and held it out to her. "The house needs a lot of work after a decade as a plant nursery. Brian and Laney might take one look at it and decide they'd rather buy something in better shape."

Christine took a sip of her coffee. "That's true." She sipped again as if drawing strength from the espresso. "Thank you for talking me off the ledge. I'm still unhappy, but it doesn't seem so bad now." She set her cup down and reached into her purse. "I'm still suspicious of the Farrells, but like you said, it's not as if they're going to take possession of the house tomorrow."

Debbie went over to the cash register. "I don't blame you for getting upset over the news. We were all excited when we heard about the plan for the Dennison House."

"It would be a perfect fit for this area." Christine handed Debbie her credit card. "One thing I do take comfort in is knowing that Chad and Theresa won't be lowballed by anyone, no matter what kind of connection a buyer claims to have. The house might be in bad shape, but it's historic and in a prime location for tourism and local events. Chad and Theresa also have Rodd Nickles as their Realtor. He's not only the best Realtor in town, but Rodd's wife used to be on the preservation society's board."

Janet was tempted to ask if that might be considered a conflict of interest. But now didn't seem like a good time. They'd just calmed Christine. "The Graysons are smart people. If Laney and Brian are being dishonest, I'm sure the truth will come out."

Christine took a pen from the cup beside the register and briskly signed her receipt. "You're right about that." She dropped the pen back into the cup. "Besides the fact that we know Abe Halner never lived in the Townsends' house, anyone could've written a note on the back of a photo." She flung her purse over her shoulder. "Thank you for letting me unload, ladies. I need to get to the next thing on my to-do list."

Janet waved to Christine and watched her leave. She recalled Laney's blue spiral notebook and the black-and-white photo of the Townsend house. "You know, Christine does have a point. Anyone could make up a story about a dead grandfather who wanted them to be able to buy the house he called home."

"I know. It is rather suspicious when I think about it. Let's say Laney's grandpa is related to the couple who bought the house when it went up for auction in the forties. He wouldn't call it home unless he spent a lot of time there, in which case people like Ray and Harry would remember him."

Janet knew she needed to head home to prepare for the workshop, but Christine's visit had distracted her. "I'd wondered if Abe could have been one of the boarders after the war, possibly for such a short time that Harry and Ray never met him. But he wrote that he left Dennison in 1943."

"Unless he wrote 1943 by mistake," Debbie said. "I still catch myself writing last year's date occasionally, and this year is almost over."

"So do I." Janet reviewed every detail she could remember about their visit with Brian and Laney Farrell. She kept landing on the same point. "But Laney said her grandfather never lived in Dennison that she knew of. If it was important enough to him for some reason that he labeled it *Home* on the picture, wouldn't he have mentioned Dennison to his family at some point?"

"Maybe Christine is right about Brian and Laney trying to gain sympathy," Debbie suggested, though her tone signaled that she didn't want to believe it. "You know what they say. People don't get away with such things by acting shifty. They do it by being friendly. Finding common ground like claiming to be new empty nesters in a café run by two middle-aged women."

Janet picked up her tote bag. She had to get going if she didn't want to be late. "If the Farrells would make up a story to win over a couple preparing to sell a house, what else might they be up to?" The photo looked so real. It was real. Ray had confirmed it. "And how did they get the picture of Jonas Townsend's house in the first place?"

CHAPTER SIX

While packing a vintage FOOD—DON'T WASTE IT! shopping bag she'd found for the rationing challenge, Janet tried to imagine a scenario for how the Farrells could have gotten the picture. She was so distracted that she almost forgot to grab butter out of her refrigerator.

"Focus," she told herself. "Forget about the Farrells for now."

She made it to the middle school with everything she needed, including the confidence of knowing Debbie and Patricia were rooting for her, and that she had something unexpected in store for the students.

Janet set a small container of sugar in the center of the teacher's worktable in the Culinary Arts room. "Imagine it's 1942. Your father is fighting in the war, either in Europe or in the Pacific, and your mother has gone to work as a machinist to support the war effort." She took a stick of butter out of her bag and set it beside the sugar. "You are now in charge of doing the baking for your family of four— you, your mom, and two siblings."

Bethany scribbled frantically in her notebook.

Ana perked up. "I would gladly do that if it got me out of being in charge of my brother all afternoon."

"It does sound like a pretty fun job for someone who likes to bake, doesn't it? Except for one tiny complication. Does anyone know what families were asked to do after America entered World War II?" She held up the sugar and butter as hints.

Bethany raised her hand. "Rationing?"

"That's exactly right. Sugar and butter were imported from parts of the world impacted by the war, and the military had priority when it came to the limited amount that was available. The average person learned to live on less, which included ration books." She plunked down the sugar and butter. "This represents the amount of sugar that each person could have per week. A half pound of sugar and a quarter pound of butter. They could apply for additional sugar rations for canning season."

Ana's gaze zeroed in on the butter and sugar. "Is that the amount per family or per person?"

"Per person. But remember, people didn't rely on store-bought bread and cookies the way we do now. They did their own baking. And think about all the things we enjoy putting butter on. Toast, pancakes, popcorn—it adds up fast. And just because they could have that amount doesn't mean it was always available. Canned goods and packaged foods were rationed as well, along with coffee and other fats, including margarine and cooking oil."

"Mr. Franklin told me his mom used to bring home a white slab of margarine," Julian said. "It came with a packet of yellow dye that she kneaded into the margarine to make it the color of butter."

A girl at the next table grimaced. "That's gross."

"Not as gross as lard. Mr. Franklin told me about that too. He had it in sandwiches."

"Ew." The girl made gagging sounds.

Miranda stood up.

Janet caught her eye and subtly shook her head. She had it under control. "Back to the story. If you were a teenager living during World War II, and you were in charge of the baking, you would need to make your family's rationed sugar, butter, and margarine last. What if someone in the family has a birthday? Or your mom tells you Grandma is coming for Sunday dinner? You would learn to be creative when making desserts."

She waited for a reaction, but every student in the room sat silently taking in her illustration. Even Bethany had stopped writing notes.

"So, we're going to have a contest," Janet went on. "Each of you will come up with an original version of a World War II-era baking recipe. You can make anything you want as long it was popular during World War II, which will require some research, and you can only use ingredients that could be purchased with rationing coupons for one person."

Janet noticed how many sets of eyes were glued to the one stick of butter and small container of sugar and added, "You have three weeks to prepare. A teenager in the forties might keep a special occasion in mind and save some of their rations."

A boy at the table in the back corner asked, "What does the winner get?"

"The winner will get a gift card and have their creation for sale in the Whistle Stop Café for the last week of September. Profits from the sale of the winner's baked delight will support the Culinary Arts Club."

Miranda joined Janet up front. "This is perfect. Each year we do a special community service project. This year, the kids voted to make dinner for the residents at Good Shepherd Retirement Center at Thanksgiving. The funds can go toward that."

The students' faces suddenly seemed a lot less threatening than the day before. "So, what do you think?" Janet asked. "Are you up for the challenge?"

"Yeah!" they chorused.

"I'm glad to hear it. Today, we will practice with one of the most versatile desserts that can be made with little or no sugar. Fruit turnovers."

Janet brought out the fruit filling options she'd prepared— apple, pear, and berries. Next, she presented a row of spices. She reached into her apron pocket for a stack of index cards that Debbie had given her before she left the café. Debbie had divided each card into fourths with a marker. "For the contest, you'll each bake your own entry. But for today, for the sake of time and limited oven space, you'll work in your table groups." Janet went around and set a card on each table. "This card is your ration book. Each square allows you to take one tablespoon of sugar, butter, or another baking fat."

Ana squinted at her group's card. "This is it? For the whole group?"

"That's it."

"But this means our turnovers can only have like two table-spoons each of butter and sugar."

"That's right. But remember, fruit has natural sugar. I saw a turnover recipe online with no added sugar. And you can use as many spices as you want. I brought cinnamon, nutmeg, cloves, ginger, and allspice." Janet gestured to the bottles. "And I'll teach you how to make a simple pastry for the crust. Now for the fun part. The group that uses the least amount of sugar and fat today wins a prize—free cookies." She held up her coupons from the café and fanned them out like playing cards.

Janet waited for the girl to lodge a full-on complaint about how hard it would be to make a turnover with so little sugar and butter that actually tasted good.

But instead, Ana smiled. "Challenge accepted, Mrs. Shaw."

The next morning, Janet set Patricia's daily peppermint mocha in front of her. "I have never tasted so many creative turnovers in one sitting. Julian's group made an apple cider spice turnover with the help of zest from an orange from Julian's lunch. That was to die for. We also had a gluten-free cherry version, which I know isn't authentic, but it was creative and thoughtful."

Patricia stirred her mocha. "Did anyone manage to have unused rations and win your prize?"

"Actually, they all had some left. The winning group made peach-berry turnovers using one tablespoon of butter and no sugar."

"What are you going to have them make next?"

"Good question. I'm still researching. I might need to pay Ray and Eileen a visit early this afternoon and get some suggestions."

Janet was about to go back to the kitchen when Laney and Brian came in and found a table in the back corner. Debbie took two menus to them. Janet paused in the doorway to the kitchen. She could go in and pretend she hadn't seen them. She had plenty of work to do, and after her insightful discussion with Debbie about the cleverness of those who meant to mislead people, she wanted to ignore them.

Then she noticed the notebook on the table. The notebook Laney claimed had belonged to her grandfather.

Anyone could've written a note on that picture. Anyone could have bought a notebook and started writing in it so the handwriting matched. The handwriting didn't confirm who the owner had been. If she wanted to get to the truth of how Laney and Brian Farrell ended up with a picture of a deceased soldier's house, she would need to be creative in her approach.

Janet grabbed the coffeepot and two mugs and made her way to the table, wearing her most welcoming Whistle Stop Café smile. "Good morning. Would you like some coffee?"

"Yes please," Brian and Laney replied almost in unison.

"How are you enjoying Dennison?"

Laney moved the notebook to her lap. "We love it. Since this is a mini vacation for us, we've been exploring the area. Naturally, we went through your museum. Yesterday we toured the Uhrichsville Clay Museum and found the cutest historic village. We had a picnic there. I've also been trying to find information on Grandpa Abe."

Janet filled both their mugs with coffee. "Any luck?"

Brian reached for the sugar. "Not really. We've searched for his name online and asked locals if it sounds familiar. We've found nothing so far. This afternoon, we have a meeting scheduled with Chad and Theresa Grayson to tour the house we're interested in."

"It's nice that they're willing to show you around before the house even goes on the market." What else could she ask that might reveal some useful information without annoying them or arousing suspicion if they were up to no good?

She couldn't think of a thing, so she left the Farrells to Debbie. Janet kept her eye on them while she chatted with Patricia. When Debbie handed over another customer's order, Janet went to the kitchen to prepare a veggie scramble and eggs Benedict. The Farrells had gotten breakfast at the Pullman, so they stuck to coffee and shared a doughnut.

They didn't seem overly upset by hitting a brick wall in their search for information about Abe Halner.

She handed the finished plates to Debbie and used the opportunity to check in on the Farrells. Brian had moved his chair closer to Laney's, and Grandpa Abe's notebook was between them. When Debbie delivered their breakfast, they barely looked up from the page.

Janet kept busy filling breakfast orders while speculating about the Farrells and the puzzling Grandpa Abe. Maybe he was one of Jonas Townsend's relatives, or a close friend. As a kid, she'd thought one of her friends had five brothers when the girl only had two. The extra boys were cousins who spent so much time at the house they were often mistaken for brothers. Maybe Abe was Jonas's cousin who had felt so at home in the house that he considered it home and noted that in the picture. He could have gone by a nickname at the time, which would explain why Ray and Harry didn't remember the name Abe Halner.

Her curiosity drew her out of the kitchen, over to the coffee carafe, and across the dining room to Brian and Laney's table, where she casually offered them refills and sneaked a glance at the notebook. All she caught was, *If you ever wondered why I can't stomach pork and beans or canned spaghetti to this day, research K-rations.*

Laney looked up at Janet and pulled the notebook to her chest.

"More coffee?" Janet asked, trying to keep her tone light.

"No thanks. I'm good."

Brian cleared his throat and fidgeted in his chair. "We're ready for the check."

"Sure thing. I'll have Debbie bring it."

She felt Brian's eyes following her as she put the coffee carafe back under the brewer. Debbie slipped behind her with a tray of empty plates.

"The Farrells are ready for their check," Janet told her.

"I'll take it right over."

The clink of plates mingled with Laney and Brian's conversation. Janet pushed open the door to the kitchen as a chair scraped against the floor.

"Hang on a sec," Laney said. "I need to put away Grandpa's notebook."

Brian let out an exasperated sigh. "We have to find something more convincing."

Janet frowned. More convincing of what, exactly? And why did they need to convince anyone of anything?

Brian's words continued to replay in Janet's mind as she drove to Good Shepherd Retirement Center before leading her last workshop for the week.

Maybe Christine was right about them trying to win over Chad and Theresa. But why would they feel the need to do that?

She pulled into the picturesque grounds of the center and rolled down her car window for a dose of September air. The first day of fall was a week and a half away, so she wanted to enjoy as much of the remaining summer days as possible. For that reason, she'd chosen to have the kids make honey ice cream, straight from a 1942 ration cookbook. She would bring plenty of ration-friendly flavor options. The process used coffee cans and was designed for small children, but it would be fun. At least she hoped they'd feel that way. Debbie had even donated an industrial-size jar of honey from the café. All Janet needed to do was stop at the grocery store for rock salt, crushed ice, and light cream after a quick visit with Eileen and Ray. She took two to-go cups out of her cup holder and carried them toward the center.

Janet found Eileen and Ray on the porch enjoying the sunshine. "Hello, you two. Isn't it a gorgeous day?"

Eileen closed her eyes and breathed in deeply. "It sure is. I love this time of year."

Janet set the cups on one of the small porch tables. She hugged Eileen and then Ray. While pulling a chair closer, she caught Ray watching Eileen like a lovesick teenager. Janet smiled. The two had been inseparable for months. *Ray, come on. Just ask her out. I'm sure there's an activity coming up at Good Shepherd that you can take her to. A movie night, an ice cream social. You would be perfect together.*

Limited time and a desire not to mortify Ray kept her silent. She'd come on a mission. "I thought I'd stop by and say hello on my way to the middle school."

Eileen reached out and patted Janet's knee. "How sweet of you. It's always nice to have surprise visits."

Ray moved his wheelchair a little closer. "And to see your happy face."

Janet reached into her tote bag and withdrew two paper bags. "I come bearing goodies. Chocolate chip cookies, fresh out of the oven, and milk in the to-go cups."

Eileen accepted her bag and selected one of the cups. "Now I'm glad I passed on dessert at lunch."

Ray took out his cookie, his eyes gleaming. "I didn't pass on dessert, and I'm still eating this. Life is too short not to have dessert at every opportunity."

Janet set her tote bag beside her chair. She leaned back and crossed one leg over the other, taking a moment to enjoy the chorus of birdsong that serenaded her and her friends from a nearby tree. Then she got down to business. "I must confess that I came for another reason too."

Ray broke off a big chunk of cookie. "You can come with any hidden agenda you want if you show up with snacks. Might this be about the Townsends? I haven't been able to get Jonas out of my head since that couple came into the café."

Eileen set her cup of milk on the table beside her. "What's on your mind, my friend?"

"I'm sure Ray filled you in on the preservation society's plan to buy the old Townsend house, as well as the couple that showed up at the café with a photo of it."

"He did. What crazy timing, isn't it?" Eileen glanced at Ray. "What did you say the woman's grandfather's name was? Abe something or other?"

Ray finished chewing and washed down his bite with some milk. "Halner."

"I know Jonas Townsend was the last member of his family to have rightful ownership of the house," Janet said. "Is it possible that he had a cousin who thought of the house as home as well?"

Ray took the napkin out of his bag and brushed crumbs from his slacks. "Jonas didn't have any family other than his parents. They had no siblings, and neither did Jonas. He always envied the kids who had brothers and sisters to fight with, plus big family gatherings on holidays."

Janet thought about all the fun she had with her cousins. "It must have been so lonely."

"He never complained about being lonely, though I think he felt it. I think the harder thing for Jonas was being poor."

"But he lived in such a nice house."

Eileen patted her mouth with her napkin. "Because his father inherited it."

"Larry Townsend had a habit of losing money on business ideas that went nowhere and get-rich-quick schemes," Ray explained. "If not for the war, Jonas planned to go to college and create a more stable life for himself with Gracie Pike."

"Eileen, did you know Jonas?"

"Very well. Gracie too. I was a couple years ahead of them in school, but it was hard to miss the two of them walking around town. They were so in love. It was tragic what happened to Jonas and his parents. It devastated the entire community."

Her friends' expression and the word *tragic* sent a chill through Janet's body. "What happened to his parents? I mean, I know they died in some kind of accident, but I never heard details."

Eileen grimaced. "It was a car accident. The brakes failed on their car. It happened a little after midnight on the interstate, shortly after Jonas shipped off to Europe. Heaven knows where they were headed at that time of night."

Ray's eyes were filled with a deep sadness. "I heard about it through my mother. I didn't find out about Jonas's death until I returned to Dennison after the war ended. I lost touch with Jonas after he was stationed in Italy while I was sent to Holland. It was hard enough to find out that Jonas's parents died, but to lose Jonas too—I was heartbroken. Even now, it feels like a bad dream."

Eileen seemed to have forgotten about her cookie. "When Jonas's parents died, his girlfriend had to break the news to him in a letter. Poor girl."

Janet drummed her fingers on the armrest of the wicker chair. "I guess Debbie and I can eliminate the possibility of Abe Halner being Jonas Townsend's cousin from our list of ideas for who he could be. I'm sorry, Ray. It feels wrong to bring all of this up when it's so painful for you."

Ray patted her hand. "Now don't you worry about a tough old thing like me, Janet. I know you're trying to find answers about a situation that seems to have something to do with my friend. Besides,

I'd rather have a little pain talking about him than keep it all to myself and feel like no one else misses him. Ask me whatever you need to."

Janet nodded. She would trust his self-assessment. "In that case, are you sure it was Jonas's bicycle that you saw beside the garage in Laney's photo?"

"Positive. I saw a tear in the seat that he'd mended with electrical tape. I was with him when he discovered the tear. It was small, but he didn't want it to get worse, so I lent him the tape."

One more possibility could lift the cloud of suspicion from Laney and Brian Farrell's arrival in Dennison, even though she had all but eliminated it based on the dates alone. "One idea I came up with is that Abe Halner might have stayed in the boardinghouse after the war."

He frowned, considering the idea. "That name doesn't ring a bell at all. I used to spend a lot of time at the boardinghouse visiting the other veterans. I don't like to be one to make assumptions without having all the facts, but I hope that couple isn't up to something fishy."

Janet tried to put all the speculations that she, Ray, and Eileen had come up with out of her mind for the sake of fifteen middle schoolers. But as she drove toward Dennison Middle School and approached the street where the house that used to belong to Jonas Townsend and his parents stood, the possibilities started swimming around in her head again.

Laney's grandfather might have had dementia. He had been ninety-eight, after all.

The picture could have belonged to someone else, maybe a friend, and somehow made its way into Grandpa Abe's notebook.

Perhaps Grandpa Abe had a pattern of making up stories about his life.

And then there was Eileen's last idea before Janet had to say goodbye. "People sell vintage photos at garage sales and antique shops all the time. I once bought a photograph of a pretty girl in a 1920s-style dress because I got a kick out of the sassy expression on her face. Maybe someone in Grandpa Abe's family bought the picture because they liked old houses. It could even be from Jonas's parents' belongings. If they didn't have relatives in the area and the house went up for auction after Jonas was reported killed, their belongings could have easily made the rounds through multiple thrift shops."

When she reached the Victorian home, Janet saw Laney and Brian on the brick walkway engrossed in a conversation with Chad and Theresa Grayson. Laney was showing Chad and Theresa something in her grandfather's notebook.

Janet kept driving, even though everything in her wanted to stop and give the Farrells the third degree once and for all. She remembered Eileen's point about photos that wound up in thrift shops. She could easily imagine Laney in a cute little thrift shop in Lakewood, thumbing through a box of old photos, thinking how perfect vintage pictures would be on the walls when she finally had her themed B and B. In her mind's eye, Laney paused at a small square photo of a house between paper-framed portraits of unsmiling families from the turn of the twentieth century. If she and Brian wanted an old house to turn into a B and B, they would've been searching online for homes that were vacant or already for sale. She imagined Laney seeing *Home, Dennison, Ohio* on the back and then doing an online search with Brian. How could they win over the seller?

Janet pulled into the school parking lot. *You don't have any proof that Laney found the photo in a store and came up with a scheme to gain favor with the Graysons.*

But how else would Laney end up with a picture of someone else's family home?

CHAPTER SEVEN

Naples, Italy
October 20, 1943

Jonas pushed franks and beans around on his tin plate with a fork. The only thing motivating him to eat the food in front of him was the need to keep up his strength for battle. He'd been lucky enough to get a chocolate bar with his meal. But lately, everything tasted the same—like nothing. Since Gracie's letter a week before, his life had become a blurry fog of doing what he had to do to survive and not thinking about the truth of what had happened.

Or what had really happened.

He couldn't erase the image of the sheet of V-Mail with Gracie's A-plus penmanship and none of her usual hearts.

Dearest Jonas,

I am desperately sorry to share this news in a letter. There was no other way to reach you, other than a telegram, and what I have to tell you requires far more words than a telegram allows.

On that night in his tent with Gracie's words in front of him, Jonas had braced himself for a Dear John letter. Practically every week, one of his fellow soldiers received one from a girl who'd decided she simply couldn't stand the idea of waiting for a boy who might not come home.

A Dear John letter would have been far easier to bear than Gracie's news. He would have felt at least slightly prepared for it, even if she had promised to wait for him and accepted his informal marriage proposal.

Jonas stabbed his fork into a mini frankfurter and forced himself to chew and swallow it. To focus on his next mission.

Not on Mom and Dad.

The brakes failing on the interstate.

The words killed instantly *in Gracie's handwriting and the teardrop stains that smeared the line below those awful words.*

His father had cared for that Ford meticulously. So meticulously that Jonas had often caught himself wishing Dad would be as careful with the family's bank account.

How could the brakes have failed? Where were they going? Gracie's letter said the accident happened after midnight. They never went for rides late at night. Mom didn't like it.

"Keep them out of this."

"I told you he couldn't be trusted."

If only he knew the identity of "he." Not that he could do anything if he did know. Not from Italy.

A hand on his shoulder broke Jonas out of his trance.

"How are you today, Jonas?" The short wiry man everyone called Chip—due to a chipped front tooth that his parents could never afford to have fixed—sat beside him on the ground with a tin bowl of spaghetti and meat sauce.

Jonas scooped up a forkful of beans. "Yeah, I'm okay. Thanks for asking."

Chip moved a little closer. He watched out for all the younger recruits, being nearly thirty with a wife and son back home. He'd been the first to reach out when he learned of Gracie's news. "You know, if you talk to the sergeant, I bet he can arrange for some leave. It's your parents."

Jonas fought the growing lump in his throat. He did want to go home. He had probably missed his parents' burial, but he longed to be able to relax enough to grieve properly, to be in familiar surroundings with the comfort of familiar people. To hold a proper funeral.

But they were at war.

"He offered," Jonas said. "They don't have any family to plan a service. Mom's folks are gone, and Dad's parents are way out in Oregon. They would want me to stick it out and honor them properly after all this is over."

And when it is, I will find out why Dad's brakes really failed.

When he and Ray had enlisted, he expected to be overseas for a short time. Now the war seemed to be dragging on forever. It felt strange to be in Italy, a place that had sounded so exotic in school. It didn't seem exotic now.

He didn't need anything he'd learned in French class.

Chip offered him a cup of black coffee. "Listen, if you ever need anything, or to talk, let me know, okay? We may be fighting a war, but you're still a human being."

"Thanks." Jonas accepted the coffee. It was real coffee, not a substitute like at home. He almost told Chip everything. About his dad's series of failed businesses. The many reasons why he thought his parents' car accident hadn't been an accident at all.

But one thing he appreciated about military life was how little the other guys knew about him or his family. He was Private Townsend, who planned to marry his pretty girlfriend back home. He didn't have to explain why his dad's shop had gone under, or why he lived in a nice house but still had to work for every extra plus some necessities. Telling Chip that he thought someone might have rigged his dad's car would make him sound paranoid unless he told everything else too.

That his father might have gotten himself into big trouble.

He could tell Ray when they both made it home. Ray might even help him figure out what had happened.

CHAPTER EIGHT

Patricia peeled the wrapper off the blueberry muffin she'd ordered with her morning mocha. "How did the honey ice cream work out?"

"It was a hit. We didn't have time to freeze it completely, so it was basically soft serve, but the kids didn't care." Janet was thankful to have a weekend to figure out the solution to her biggest dilemma related to the Culinary Arts Club contest. "I don't know how I'm going to choose a best rationing-era baked treat from this group."

Debbie came over with an order and handed it to Janet. "No cooking required on this one. They ordered one cinnamon roll and one scone. Would you get those? I'll get started on their coffees."

Greg came in as Janet was handing the plates of treats across the counter to Debbie.

Debbie quickly delivered the order and came back. "Good morning. Another big day on the home renovation site?"

Greg said hello to Patricia and went over to peer into the bakery case. "If things keep going as they have been, I'll be able to put it up for sale by mid-October. That is, if I can avoid getting too derailed by the latest drama with the Townsend house. Christine Murray wants to call a special emergency chamber of commerce meeting."

Janet glanced over at Debbie. "An emergency meeting over a house?"

"Yes indeed. She sent a warning about the Farrells and wants to discuss how to handle the situation. She's convinced they're using that old picture to be manipulative and wants us to find some kind of evidence to disprove their claim that Laney Farrell's grandfather might have a connection to it."

Patricia pinched off a chunk of muffin. "I know I don't have the full scoop on what's going on, but it's not illegal to claim to have a connection to a house. Even if the sellers do favor them because of it, that kind of thing happens all the time. Does Christine plan to put everyone who shows interest in the house through the same wringer?"

Greg requested a muffin from the bakery case. "Good point, Patricia."

Even with her own suspicions about Laney and Brian, Janet thought Christine was taking things too far. Janet had mulled over the whole thing while going to sleep and finally accepted that, even if Brian and Laney had come to town with a made-up story and a picture from a thrift store, she couldn't prove it. To Patricia's point, it would be wrong but not against the law. And when she took a moment and thought about it, they didn't seem like the deceptive type. "An emergency meeting is way over the top, isn't it?"

"I know, but I guess the Farrells and the Graysons really hit it off. They connected over stories about their grandfathers. Laney's grandfather fought in World War II. Chad's grandfather did as well, but was listed as missing in action, and his family never learned what happened to him. So naturally, they had a lot to talk about."

Debbie picked up a tip that someone had left on a table. "In the end, a house usually goes to the highest bidder, not the one with the most heartwarming story. Maybe the possibility of the preservation society being outbid is hitting Christine. Even though we have no idea what the Farrells' financial situation is, and the society might qualify for grants and such that wouldn't be available to private citizens."

Greg asked for a coffee to go with his muffin then said, "Possibly. Between you and me, I think Christine is more concerned with losing control over what happens to the house and her plan for the museum than with knowing the story behind Brian and Laney's photo. Even before they entered the scene, she seemed possessive of the project." He walked over to the cash register and took out his wallet. "And now Rodd is upset because, as he put it, he doesn't want what should be a cut-and-dried process disrupted by anyone's need to dig up the past."

Janet found the largest, most perfect muffin for Greg.

Debbie poured him a large coffee. "How strange that the other day we were all excited about plans for the Dennison House, and now everything is on hold because of a very nice couple with a picture and grandpa story."

Greg took two cups of creamer from a basket on the counter. "I saw Rodd at the gym last night, pumping weights like he was preparing for a bodybuilding competition. I stopped to joke with him about his intensity level, and he said he was working off some frustration after Chad Grayson texted him the picture from Laney's grandfather's notebook. I asked what the big deal was. He said the image included something that could complicate more than the home sale, but he couldn't talk about it. I've never seen him so stressed."

Patricia crumpled her muffin wrapper. "You'd think he'd be thrilled over a possible bidding war. The Graysons could get more than the asking price with two parties eager to buy the house before it has even gone on the market. That means a bigger commission for Rodd."

"You'd think. He said he would pull out of involvement in the sale if Christine, the Farrells, or anyone else insists on researching the house's past. And he flat-out refuses to participate in Christine's emergency meeting."

Patricia got up and handed her credit card to Debbie. "That doesn't sound like the Rodd I know. There must be more to the story. In my opinion, this could backfire on Christine if she pushes too hard on questioning the Farrells and turns out to be wrong. As an attorney, I would advise her not to go around spreading rumors without evidence."

Janet avoided eye contact with Patricia for fear that, as an attorney, she might see in her eyes that she hadn't been sure about the Farrells either the day before. "Whether the place becomes the Dennison House or the Farrells' themed bed and breakfast, this could turn out to be an interesting real estate saga."

Janet was still pondering Greg's update when she went out to the bakery counter midmorning with a fresh tray of molasses cookies and saw Laney walking into the café by herself.

Instead of finding a table, Laney took a seat at the counter.

Janet set the tray on the counter and opened the bakery case. All her suspicions about Laney had evaporated. In fact, she felt silly for getting sucked into Christine's theatrics. "Good morning, Laney. Where's Brian? Sleeping in?"

"No, he's on a video call for work. Something came up that he couldn't get out of. Then we're heading home to Lakewood. I'm coming back on Monday for a few days by myself. I want to know the story behind Grandpa Abe's house. Or his picture of a house, that is. Rodd Nickles—the Realtor that the Graysons plan to use—stopped by while we were touring the house. He suggested I should let all this go and accept that we might never know why Grandpa wrote what he did on the picture. But I don't think I can."

"I don't blame you. I wouldn't be able to either." The idea of Rodd telling a complete stranger to let go of innocent questions about a family member's history didn't sit well with Janet. It was Rodd's job to sell the house fairly, not to chase off potential buyers. At best, that seemed downright self-sabotaging. Besides, what business of his was it if someone wanted to know more about a large financial investment before they took the plunge?

"I've already talked to Kim Smith, and the Pullman we're staying in was available all next week, so I booked it. I'm excited to spend more time here. Everyone has been so welcoming, especially you and Debbie."

Janet's stomach clenched with guilt, but she covered her embarrassment with a smile. "What are you hoping to find?"

Laney shrugged. "I wish I knew. It fascinates me that we never knew more about Grandpa's life. When I read his notebook, I feel like—I don't know, like he was trying to tell us something but passed away before he could." She took the notebook out of her tote bag and opened it to show Janet. "See? They're random sentences and paragraphs, each one on a separate page as if he planned to write more details later but didn't want to lose the thought. My sister is a writer, and this is how some of her notebooks look when she's brainstorming a new book."

Janet read the page.

Belgium 1945.
Tell them about the family.

"That could be brainstorming notes. I take it he wasn't the kind of grandpa who told 'when I was a boy' stories, or sat around rehashing old memories while drinking instant coffee."

Laney laughed. "Not really. I know his parents died when he was young. When I asked how, he always said, 'That's a story for another time. When you're older.' I know he fought in Europe during World War II, but he was never one to tell war stories or even get involved in veterans groups. I always assumed he didn't want to talk about sad things. Once I asked to interview him for a school history project, and he encouraged me to interview Grandma instead, claiming that her stories from the war years were better. 'More suitable for children,' he said."

Janet, who had heard and read some of the more horrific stories from soldiers during World War II, had to agree with Abe's assessment.

Laney picked up a menu. "Grandma's family took in a little girl who'd been evacuated from London during the Blitz, and the two of them organized a neighborhood victory garden. The story was so intriguing that I never thought to question Grandpa passing me off to her for it. He was such a loving, fun, and hardworking man that it was easy to excuse his being private about the past as a generational thing."

The café was in a rare lull, so Janet offered Laney a cup of coffee. Now that it was just the two of them talking about her grandfather, all suspicions about Laney's motives faded into the air with the fragrances of bacon and coffee from the breakfast rush. Laney didn't come across as a woman trying to get away with something. She seemed more interested in learning about her grandfather than in acquiring a house through fraudulent means.

Janet took Laney's order for half an eggs Benedict and side of fruit then left her to chat with Debbie. When Janet returned from the kitchen, Laney was flipping pages in the blue spiral notebook.

"Find anything interesting?"

She set the book aside. "Brian and I have read through these pages a dozen times, and we always end up just as confused as we were the first time. As if we're reading about a different person than the one I knew all my life. Take this for example." Laney flipped to another page. "'I covered Chip and left the dugout. I didn't even have time to say a prayer. Chip was from Philly. A good man.'"

"And?"

"And that's it. Here's another one. 'If you want to know the real me, it's in SDB105 Capital.'"

Debbie came over to join them. "Sorry to eavesdrop, but I heard what you said, and it was really cryptic."

Laney shut the notebook and pushed it aside. "It is. Grandpa Abe wasn't a cryptic person. Then there's the key that could go to anything, but fits nothing I've tried so far, including the Townsend house."

The longer Janet stood behind the counter and listened to Laney talk about what she remembered about her grandfather—his knack for fixing cars, how he turned into a big kid at Christmas and loved all the chaos of grandkids at the house, his ability to read and speak French fluently even though his family of origin was Swedish, his determination to keep up with technology even into his nineties— the more Janet wanted to help her find out how a picture of Jonas Townsend's family home ended up in Abe Halner's notebook.

Laney had become more than a tourist who wanted to buy a house to turn into a B and B. She was a woman who had come to Dennison looking for answers. And Janet was determined to help her find them.

CHAPTER NINE

*S*haring a pizza and salad with her husband, Police Chief Ian Shaw, at Buona Vita felt like the perfect way to end the week. Now that they were both full and happy, with tasty leftovers for lunch the next day, Janet was ready to figure out her next step for the Culinary Arts Club.

"My plan for this weekend is to come up with a strategy for how to choose the best recipe for my contest. I never expected it to be this hard. Plus, I'm seeing a whole new side of Julian. I knew he was a smart kid, but he's creative as well. Two days in a row, he found ways to use leftovers from his lunch as a flavor enhancer. First the orange zest for the turnovers and then broken-up pretzels in his group's ice cream. Talk about making do."

"Yum." Ian licked his lips. "Sweet-and-salty ice cream. I want a sample of that."

"You want a sample of any dessert. I'll see if I can replicate it." Her husband had a major sweet tooth. She opened the to-go box their waiter had left at the end of the table. "If I didn't know it would break the bank and defeat the purpose of challenging these kids with the rationing recipes, I would present all of them with gift cards and a place of honor in the bakery case at the café."

"You should pitch a baking competition show." Ian held up the fork from his salad like a microphone. "Fifteen thirteen- and fourteen-year-olds with talent that rivals the pros. The perfect recipe for success—or so it seems. Janet's young bakers may be up to the challenge of World War II rationing. But will the kitchen survive adolescent hormones?"

Janet laughed and playfully shoved her husband's shoulder. "You goof. Although a professional-level competition might become necessary at the rate these kids are going. I could hire Harry as a judge." *Harry. Yes.* She slid the remaining four slices of pizza into the box.

"Why are you smiling? Are you going to try the baking show idea? I was joking."

Janet shut the cardboard box and patted the top. "No way. I don't want to be on television. But I do have an idea. Before I get too excited about it, I need to discuss it with Debbie."

Ian grabbed the box. "Ready to go home?"

"Yep." Janet took her sweatshirt off the back of the chair. While pulling it on, she spotted Rodd Nickles at the cash register picking up a takeout order. "We aren't the only ones who thought Italian food sounded good tonight."

Rodd looked over his shoulder and glanced at Ian.

"Hey, Rodd. How are you doing?" Ian asked.

"Doing all right. Thanks."

Janet expected Rodd to come over to talk for a few minutes. That was common practice in a town like Dennison, where almost everyone had grown up together, and the Realtor never missed an opportunity to socialize.

But Rodd paid for his order and left.

Janet zipped her sweatshirt. "Well, that was different." Not that it completely shocked her after Greg's recap of Rodd's workout at the gym.

"Yeah. He seemed a bit off."

"Maybe it's about the Townsend house. It sounds like he has his work cut out for him with Christine Murray. And according to Greg Connor, he isn't happy about it. I think he expected an ordinary cut-and-dried sale."

Ian opened his wallet and took out some cash for a tip. "I wouldn't expect something like that to affect an experienced Realtor like Rodd. I'm sure Christine isn't the first overzealous potential buyer he's dealt with. I wonder what's up with him."

An hour after Ian fell asleep, Janet lay wide awake on her side of the bed with the events of the week bouncing around in her mind. In typical late-night fashion, the encounter with Rodd grew bigger and bigger until she was convinced there must be more to his quick exit than simply being in a hurry.

Unable to shut off her imagination, she got up, took her phone to the living room, and typed in the search bar, *when people you know start behaving strangely.*

She yawned halfway through a story about a woman who found out her sweet elderly neighbor was a serial killer. She was pretty sure that was not what was going on with Rodd.

Her dark gray cat, Ranger, hopped on the couch and curled up on her lap.

"Don't get too comfy, Ranger," Janet whispered. "I'm heading back to bed before I click my way any deeper down the black hole."

She tapped away from the article and was about to power off her phone when another link drew her right back into her screen with the words *Dennison, Ohio* and *unsolved*.

I'm going to be sorry I stayed up reading when my alarm goes off in a few hours.

But from the first sentence of the article, she knew she wouldn't be able to sleep at all until she finished it. How was it possible that she'd lived in Dennison her whole life and never knew these things happened there?

Debbie tied her apron in back. "You read all that because Rodd didn't come over to chat?"

Janet took a flat of eggs out of the refrigerator and set it on the counter near the griddle. "To be fair, Ian also found it odd when Rodd hightailed it out of Buona Vita." She followed Debbie out to the dining room to help with last-minute tasks so they could open. Saturdays were always hectic.

Debbie picked up an order pad and pen from beside the cash register. "I'm sure I would've found it strange, but I can't say I'd lose sleep over it. Besides, it's not as if we've ever had a reason to speculate about Rodd Nickles or anyone in his family. He is a respected member of the community. When his wife, Gretta, served on the preservation society board, she rivaled Christine in her ability to get funding for projects. Their kids are nice, successful people. His grandkids are stars of every sports team and dance troupe they participate in."

"I suppose he's allowed an introverted night once in a while." Janet's comment about Rodd's grandkids prompted a recollection of the enthusiastic notetaker from Dennison Middle School. *Bethany Nickles*. Janet had seen her name on the front of her notebook. "One of his granddaughters is in the Culinary Arts Club. I don't know why I didn't make the connection until now."

"And I bet she's one of the stars."

"Definitely the most invested. She takes notes and everything."

Janet glanced toward the window for signs of early-morning customers waiting by the door before they were officially open. The coast was clear. "Before anyone shows up, I have to tell you what I found before I fell asleep on the couch. I stumbled on an old article about a crime ring that was active in Dennison back in the forties. Illegal gambling, extortion, money laundering, accidents that involved people who owed a lot of money."

Debbie flipped the sign to Open in the front window. "Did any familiar names come up in the story?"

Janet chuckled. "No. But I must say the darkness of the living room made the article an especially disturbing read. I left the house before Ian got up, so I texted it to him."

"Text it to me too. I'm intrigued." Debbie unlocked the café door. "Oh, I forgot to tell you. Christine relented. She still doesn't trust the Farrells, but she called off the emergency meeting. I have a feeling someone reminded her that if she wants the Graysons to be excited about her project, she should choose her battles wisely."

"That's a relief. When Laney came in yesterday, I felt bad for ever letting Christine's concerns sway me. Laney only wants to know more about what she found, and if her grandpa really did want her to have that house for her B and B, she would like to buy it. End of story." No one had come in yet, so Janet decided to push her luck with one more thing. "I have an idea to run past you."

"What's that?"

"I've told you what incredible bakers I have in the Culinary Arts Club, right?"

"Yeah. It's so exciting to see young people passionate about things."

"They are so good that I wasn't sure how I could fairly choose a winner for the contest we cooked up. So I've come up with something else. I have to okay it with Miranda, but I thought it might be fun to let a panel judge the contest entries instead of me. What do you think of holding the judging here at the café two Saturdays from now, right after closing time, and asking Harry, Eileen, and Ray to be the judges?"

"I love the idea, but it might be tricky to set up the judging area if customers are still in the café."

"I thought we might set up tables right outside the door, in the depot."

Debbie put her hands on her hips and peered through the front window of the café. "That might work."

"It wouldn't require much extra work on our part other than time. The kids are doing the baking. They'll have to do it at home, of course." It would be on the honor system like any other school project. "And we'll need to organize transportation for our three judges. If nothing else, I can pick them up."

Debbie grinned. "Let's do it."

"Perfect. Thank you so much." Janet hurried to the kitchen to fetch a tray of cinnamon rolls, which always went quickly on Saturdays.

Debbie opened the door for a family of four and got them settled at a table. Once she'd poured coffee for the parents and given all four of them water, she joined Janet behind the counter.

Janet slid the tray of rolls into the bakery case. "I still need to figure out the gift card. Now that I'm kicking the contest up a notch, I want the prize to reflect that."

"How about that trendy food store, Earth's Market? Greg's boys like to go there for smoothies."

"I forgot about that place now that Tiffany is away at school." Earth's Market had become popular with teenagers for their juice and smoothie bar, plus a cool selection of European and Asian snacks. Janet even remembered seeing some unique spice blends and cookie cutters there. "That would be a perfect prize for a baking contest."

"They might be willing to donate a card if you tell them what it's for."

"I'll call this afternoon."

By midmorning, Janet was down to the last cinnamon roll in the case. Fortunately, she had prepared a second tray. As she brought it out of the kitchen, she found Harry standing at the bakery case with Crosby. The dog wore a forlorn expression that clearly said, *How come there's nothing in that case for me?*

"Aw, Crosby. One of these days, I'll make you some dog cookies and put them on a special tray." Janet opened the case. "Hey, Harry. Do you want to judge a contest? There are baked goods involved."

Harry looked down at Crosby. "What do you think? My doctor told me yesterday that I need to reduce my sodium intake, but he didn't say a thing about sugar."

Cosby sat on his haunches and wagged his tail, as if offering to help judge baked goods.

"You're right, I should probably think carefully about this." Harry scratched under his chin and gazed up at the ceiling as if deep in thought. "Okay, I thought about it. Count me in. Bring on the cookies and cake."

"Great. And it's wonderful you've kept your blood sugar in check, Harry. The contest is two weeks from today if it works out as neatly in real life as in my mind. I need a few experts to decide which of my students bakes the tastiest treat using rationing restrictions."

A woman and little boy approached the bakery case, so Harry stepped aside to give them room. "After hearing the report on how the turnovers and honey ice cream turned out, I'm excited to try their creations."

Janet shut the case. "I want to invite Ray and Eileen as well. Feel free to give them a heads-up, so they can keep two weeks from today from two to about three in the afternoon open."

"I'm sure they'll be happy to keep their calendars open that day."

"Thank you. Now I hope the Culinary Arts teacher okays the idea, and that the kids can free up the time in *their* calendars."

Janet left Harry to decide what he wanted from the bakery and waited on the woman and little boy. With Laney in Lakewood for the weekend, she could pour all her extra time and energy into the contest. That way, if Laney returned with new developments, she'd be able to give them her full attention.

CHAPTER TEN

With her hours packed with contest preparation, Janet's weekend flew by.

But on Monday morning, she was able tell Debbie, "We have a contest. The manager of Earth's Market is donating a gift card that I can pick up today. Miranda agreed to the updated contest idea, and all the students are free that Saturday afternoon as long as we don't mind Bethany Nickles and Heather O'Neil coming in soccer uniforms so they can head to their game from the contest. Julian has a soccer game in the morning but promised to shower afterward."

Debbie went into the dining room with a tray of newly filled salt and pepper shakers. "I think it will be cute to have some kids in soccer uniforms."

Janet followed her to help distribute the shakers. "So do I. It will show how committed they are to take part. To make sure they don't get help with their entries, Miranda is requiring students and parents to sign an honesty contract as well as the permission slip. We will assign a number to each student's entry so the whole thing can be judged blind. That way, the judges can't be partial to anyone. I'll explain everything to the club when I follow up with them on Thursday."

"I mentioned the contest to Kim, and she's going to contribute a fun thank-you gift for your judges."

"I can't wait to see what she comes up with." Janet set two shakers on the last table.

"Me either," Debbie said. "By the way, I read the article you sent me about the crime ring. It's like something out of a movie."

"Right? When Patricia comes in, we should ask if any of it sounds familiar to her."

By seven thirty, the morning crowd was making their way in and out of the café. Patricia came in at quarter to eight, professional yet comfortable in a royal-blue cardigan and gray slacks.

Debbie took a clean mug out of the rack against the back wall. "Good morning, Patricia. How are you today?"

Paticia took a stool at the counter, halfway between the bakery case and the register. "I'm good. I have a nine o'clock client this morning and need to prepare beforehand."

While Patricia was the only customer, Janet seized the opportunity to tell her about what she had read. "Patricia, this might interest you as someone in the legal profession. Have you ever heard of the local crime ring that was active during the forties? According to what I read, the crimes mostly involved illegal gambling and extortion. Though apparently there were also accidents involving people who happened to owe large debts."

Patricia thought for a moment then said, "When I was in law school, a story came up in a discussion about circumstantial evidence. A man named Clive Baringer went to prison for money laundering and extortion. He was also a suspect in a murder in Uhrichsville. The victim was a man who owed Baringer over twenty-five hundred dollars in gambling debts. The man was found dead in his home, from a gas leak. His fiancée had a copy of a letter from Clive Baringer that threatened repercussions if he didn't receive payment by a certain date, which happened to be a week before the man died. The fiancée had also witnessed a confrontation between the two men."

"And yet they couldn't charge him with murder?" Janet guessed. As the wife of a police chief, she was all too familiar with such things.

"That's right. All the evidence was considered circumstantial. But his arrest led them to a big underground ring that involved several local men. Baringer supposedly kept a list of people who owed large debts, and a few of those people died in ways that couldn't be pinned to anyone other than circumstantially."

"During the discussion, did any of the other names come up? Other victims?" Janet asked, thinking of the Townsends' mysterious car accident.

"Not that I recall, but it's been several years since I heard about it." Patricia sipped from her mug. "Before I forget, Pop Pop told me you asked him to judge your contest. He's thrilled. If it's all right, I'd like to come and take photos."

"I see no reason why you couldn't," Janet said.

"Great. Thank you." She checked the time. "That time already? I'd better get moving."

"Sure. Let me pour that into a to-go cup for you."

After Patricia left, the café was empty, and Janet was able to fill Debbie in on what Patricia's law-school story had brought to mind. "Jonas's parents died because the brakes failed on their car," she concluded. "Eileen couldn't begin to guess what they were doing on the interstate after midnight."

Debbie moved Patricia's empty mug to the cart of dirty dishes. "But wouldn't a family member have suspected foul play if the accident seemed suspicious to them, or if Mr. and Mrs. Townsend owed a lot of money?"

Janet thought about the one person who could have possibly known whether Larry and Bridget Townsend were indebted to Clive Baringer. "Their only son was in Europe fighting in the war, and as far as I know, they didn't have other relatives. If Jonas suspected foul play, he died in battle before he got a chance to tell anyone."

Janet hung up her apron shortly after one o'clock. "Thanks for taking over, Paulette. I'm off to pick up the gift card."

"I'm glad to help." Paulette opened a new package of hamburger buns. "If you see anything new and exciting over there, let me know."

"I'll send pictures of the most tempting treats." Janet said a quick goodbye to Debbie. She was almost at the door when Laney pushed it open and nearly collided with her.

"Janet, I am so sorry." She stopped to catch her breath.

Janet put her hand on Laney's arm. "No harm done. Are you okay? You look kind of frazzled."

"Yes, I'm okay. It's just…Well, a tire blew on my car. It startled me."

"Oh no. Do you want to talk about it?"

"I think that would help, if you have time."

"Of course I do." Janet ushered Laney out of the café and toward one of the depot benches.

A group of college students came out of the museum. Their chatter over where to get something to eat and work on the assignment that had brought them to the museum bounced off the walls of the depot. It faded as they went into the café.

"Now, tell me everything," Janet said. "Do you need the contact information for our local mechanic?"

"Actually, the tire blew a block away from the shop. A man came right over to tow my car there. But it needs a new tire, and they're super busy, so they don't think they'll get to it before the end of the day."

"I'm so sorry. What a bummer."

Laney opened her tote bag. "This couldn't have happened at a worse time. I think I figured out what the key from my grandfather's notebook might open."

"What is it?"

"Last week, when the Graysons took Brian and me on a tour of the house, I asked if I could try inserting the key into the front door. It didn't fit. It's not the right size for a house key, so I knew it was a long shot. But I had to try." She reached into her tote bag and took out her grandfather's notebook and a plastic bag containing a tarnished gold key. "When I went home for the weekend, I matched it against some of my keys. My gym locker. Our storage unit." She handed it to Janet.

Janet rotated it slowly in her fingers. "It is about the right size for a storage unit or maybe a safe."

"That's what I thought. So I searched the notebook for references to a safe or storage. Nothing. I compared the key to one more that I had, the extra key to an old safe-deposit box that Brian and I used to keep important documents in. They're the exact same size."

"Then your grandfather must have had one."

"I asked Brian to check the file drawer where we put Grandpa's documents to see if his bank statements included a fee for a safe-deposit box. I also asked my mom to go through what she had. Neither found one. Not for his bank in Lakewood anyway, or in Cincinnati." She flipped the notebook open to a page near the back. "Then I remembered the entry with the series of numbers and letters and the word *capital*. At the bottom of the same page, I found this."

Janet read the note that Laney pointed to.

SDB105 Capital. Fillmore St.

"Now that I'm connecting the dots, I think the series of capital letters and numbers refers to a safe-deposit box number. Could 'Capital' be the name of a bank? If it's close, I could walk there."

"We don't have a Capital Members Bank in Dennison. I haven't heard of one anywhere in this area." Then why did the name seem familiar? She put her fingertips on her temples. *Think. I know I've heard the name.* Then it came to her. "There is a Capital Members Bank. It's been around forever and is popular with the older generation. It's on Fillmore Street in Barnhill, which is about ten minutes from here."

"That's not too far. I can call a rideshare."

Janet thought about her plan to pick up the gift cards. It was a straight shot from Earth's Market to the exit for Barnhill. "You don't need to bother with a rideshare. If you don't mind joining me on an errand, I can drive you over there."

"I can't ask you do to that."

"You didn't ask. I offered." Janet stood. "Come on."

"You don't mind?" Laney put the notebook back into her tote bag.

"Not at all. Besides, I'm intrigued."

On the drive to Earth's Market, Janet told Laney about her workshop for the Culinary Arts Club and how it had transformed into a contest at the café with authentic judges.

"That sounds like a lot of fun. I can't imagine something like that happening in the school district my kids grew up in. Don't get me wrong—the schools were great. But having a local business owner volunteer to teach a workshop that lasts more than an hour or so and then come up with something as creative as what you're doing? It would never happen. Those kids will always remember it."

"That's life in a small town for you. This one, anyway. I can't speak for all of them."

"I would love to be part of a town like this."

"Maybe you will be." Janet couldn't believe her own words. If Laney and her husband ended up in Dennison, it would be to open their B and B, which would probably mean they had outbid the Dennison Preservation Society. Meaning no Dennison House, at least at the Townsend home. *One thing at a time.*

Janet pulled up in front of Earth's Market. "Do you want to wait in the car or come in?"

"I'll come in. Maybe I'll find something to send my daughter in a care package."

Janet led the way into the store. "They have great stuff in here. My daughter loves it."

Laney wandered over to an endcap featuring new arrivals. Janet snapped a picture of the display for Paulette then went to the customer service desk to find the manager.

A twentysomething woman named Tara greeted Janet. As soon as Janet said her name, Tara opened a drawer and took out an envelope. "I'm the assistant manager, but the store manager told me to expect you. She put two cards in here. Fifty dollars for the winner, and a twenty-five-dollar card to use as a door prize or something."

Janet peeked into the envelope to make sure she'd heard Tara correctly. She saw two cardboard gift envelopes with bow designs on them. "That is so generous. Thank you."

"Her kids attended the middle school, and one of them was in the Culinary Arts Club. She said she couldn't resist."

"Please tell the manager how grateful I am. We couldn't do things like this without the community's support."

"I will. Kids are our future, so we're happy to do it."

Laney walked over with a box labeled CHOCOLATES FROM AROUND THE WORLD. "I found something. Chloe is obsessed with chocolate."

Janet put the gift cards in her tote. "That's perfect." She waited for Laney to pay for the chocolates, and then they headed back to the car.

Laney set her bag on the floor between her feet. "I was so excited for you when I heard how much the manager donated for the prize."

"I didn't expect two cards. I think I'll use the second one for an honorable mention award."

"Is that another small-town perk?"

"I think so. The whole community comes together like that all the time."

Laney snapped her fingers. "That's it. No matter what Grandpa Abe's connection is to that house, I really want to buy it so Brian and I can live here."

Goodbye Dennison House. It was nice dreaming about you. But maybe the museum could go in another old home. At that moment, sitting with Laney on their way to find Grandpa Abe's safe-deposit box, the question of who got the Townsend house didn't feel nearly as critical as helping Laney learn more about her grandfather.

CHAPTER ELEVEN

anet found Capital Members Bank with minimal help from her GPS. The 1950s-style brick structure contrasted sharply with the other businesses in the parking lot. A popular coffee shop enjoyed an early afternoon rush beside a high-end clothing store that Janet had heard about from expectant mothers. But as she watched a woman in trendy jeans stroll out of the coffee shop with a blended-ice drink and an elderly man shuffle into the bank with a folder under his arm, Janet decided the datedness of the building was part of its charm.

Laney unbuckled her seat belt. "Thanks again for giving me a ride."

"You're welcome. I can hang out in the coffee shop while you go to the bank," Janet offered.

"Actually, I'd prefer you to come with me if you don't mind. If I find something interesting, you can witness the moment."

"This could turn into an exciting Monday afternoon." Janet said a quick prayer for Laney to at least discover that the key fit.

Inside, Laney explained the situation to the teller.

Janet's heart sank a little at the teller's response. "Unless you're listed as a beneficiary or owner, I'm afraid I can't give you access to anything."

Laney pulled out her phone. "I have a photo of my grandfather's death certificate from the funeral home. Could you at least look up the box number?"

"Let me see what I can find." The teller typed some information into his computer. "What's your name?"

"Laney Farrell." She opened her wallet and took out her driver's license.

"I found a safe-deposit box under the name Abraham Halner. You're listed as a beneficiary, so I can let you see it."

Janet closed her eyes. *Yes! Thank You, God.*

Laney beamed. "Wonderful. Thank you. Can I claim the contents?"

A printer behind the teller spit out a sheet of paper. He slid it in front of Laney and handed her a pen. "Sign here, please. Since Mr. Halner has passed, feel free to take everything home with you and leave the key. I'll close the account, and the monthly payments will stop." He took a ring of keys out of a drawer.

Laney followed the teller down a hallway and motioned for Janet to join her. The teller flipped through the key ring and opened a door with a sign that read, THIS DOOR MUST REMAIN LOCKED. He held the door open for Laney and Janet.

"Once I leave, I'll lock the door for your safety. If another customer needs the room, I'll let you know." He pointed out a button beside the door. "When you're ready to go, push that and I'll come back." He found the right box and inserted a key into one of the two slots on the front. "Go ahead and put your key into the other slot."

Janet almost cheered when Laney twisted the key and the box clicked open.

"Can I bring you some coffee or water?" the teller asked.

Clutching the metal box, Laney shook her head.

"No thank you." Janet took a seat at the end of the table.

"Then I'll leave you to it."

After the teller left, Laney sat across from Janet. She stared at the box for a moment and then took a deep breath and blew out slowly. "It feels so strange to be doing this." She rested her hands on top of the lid. "Like I'm reading someone else's diary. Or breaking into a safe."

Janet said, "Technically, you've already read someone else's diary."

Laney let out a nervous chuckle. "And this is a safe. But I'm listed as a beneficiary, which means he wanted me to have whatever is in here." She hefted the box. "It seems pretty full."

"Is it heavy?"

"Not overly."

Janet wanted to urge her to open it, but Laney needed to do this in her own time. She folded her hands on the table and waited.

She didn't have to wait long. A few moments later, Laney lifted the lid and let it fall backward. "Here goes."

Janet's heart pounded as if the box contained secrets from her own family. Laney removed a lumpy folded manila envelope, secured with a thick rubber band. Next, she took out a square black velvet box that looked like it would contain jewelry, or maybe a medal of some kind. She slipped her hand to the back of the safe-deposit box and gave something a tug. Out came a drawstring bag and two smaller flat envelopes. The corner of one had torn a little. Last was a brown pocket-size New Testament with something tucked inside the front cover.

With everything out in front of her, Laney picked up the drawstring bag. "I guess I can start with this."

"Good choice."

Laney loosened the drawstring and upended the bag over her hand. A set of tarnished dog tags tumbled into her palm. Laney ran her fingers over the tags—then gasped.

Before Janet could ask what was wrong, Laney grabbed one of the smaller envelopes and tore it open. She pulled out a yellowed sheet of paper and what looked like a social security card.

Laney whispered under her breath, "This is impossible."

"What?" Janet leaned forward. "What is it? Is everything okay?"

Laney shook her head. "This can't be right." She slid the dog tags across the table. She held up the things she'd found in the envelope, her hands shaking. "This is Jonas Townsend's birth certificate and social security card."

Janet picked up the dog tags. The words were barely legible after eighty years. But the name on the birth certificate confirmed what she saw on the top tag attached to the tarnished silver ball chain. *Lieutenant Jonas C. Townsend.*

"What was my grandfather doing with Jonas Townsend's birth certificate and dog tags?"

Janet handed the tags back to Laney. "Maybe they were friends."

"Friends don't give each other their birth certificates and social security cards."

Janet's mind raced. "They could have fought together during the war. Ray Zink is ninety-eight like your grandfather, and Jonas was the same age. Maybe when Jonas was killed, your grandfather ended up with his dog tags. Or Jonas could have been captured and died in a prison camp, not in action." She'd heard stories about errors in military death records in the days before modern technology and DNA testing.

But that wouldn't explain the social security card and birth certificate.

Laney grabbed another envelope and flipped it over. It was white and had *Jonas* written across the front. Laney pulled out three sheets and unfolded them. Two were drawings done by children. The other appeared to be a letter.

"It's in French." Laney put it back in the envelope. "The drawings have some writing on them too. Also in French."

Janet almost reached for the letter but knew it wouldn't get them anywhere. "This is one of those moments when I regret taking Spanish in high school instead of French."

"And I had to go and take Japanese because I thought it sounded cool and different at the time. Also not helpful right now."

Janet tapped her fingers on the table. "What's in the big envelope?"

Laney removed the rubber band and peeked into it. "A bunch of letters and postcards."

A knock on the door made them freeze, as if they'd been caught doing something wrong.

The teller called through the door, "I have another customer waiting."

"Okay," Laney answered. "I'll be a couple minutes."

She set the fat envelope aside and picked up the Bible. She opened the cover and held it out for Janet to see. "A Gideons New Testament with the Psalms and Proverbs—and a letter."

Janet recognized the stationery from a lifetime of living in a town with roots in World War II history. "That's V-Mail. And the New Testaments were military-issued through the Gideons. Brown for army, blue for navy."

"Jonas Townsend's name is written inside the Bible. The letter is from a woman named Gracie. My grandmother's name is Ivy. I know Grandma and Grandpa met after the war, at a church potluck in St. Louis, but it's still odd that he would have kept mail from Gracie among his things." Laney glanced at the door and put the letter back into the New Testament. "Didn't your friend Ray mention a girl named Gracie when we asked him if he knew an Abe Halner?"

"Gracie Pike was Jonas's girlfriend. They planned to marry after the war."

Laney opened the velvet box and handed it to Janet. "A bracelet."

Janet fingered the gold fleur-de-lis charm dangling from the gold chain.

Laney started packing the contents of the safe-deposit box into her tote bag. "We better let the next customer have their turn. It's not as if staying here will help me figure out why Grandpa had these things." She met Janet's gaze, her eyes troubled. "I am so confused right now."

"You and me both. But we'll get it figured out," Janet said, hoping she sounded more certain than she felt.

CHAPTER TWELVE

Southern Belgium
December 28, 1944

The dugout was eerily silent when Jonas opened his eyes. His head throbbed. He tried to sit up, his teeth chattering, but a wave of nausea forced him back down again. His toes felt frozen solid in his combat boots. But when he put his hand on his forehead, it felt hot. He moved his right arm to pull the army blanket around his shoulders. Pain shot through his shoulder and down his arm. His sleeve was wet. How did I get here?

Belgium. The Bastogne region. At least he could remember that much. But how many days had it been since the battle that had sent him to where he was now? Thinking hurt his head, but he forced himself to try. He recalled an explosion that sent him flying backward. He'd woken up to pain in his arm and his shoulder, on top of a crushing headache. He'd found Chip and pulled off his coat in a vain attempt to tend a wound that looked far worse than his own. He'd dragged Chip to a dugout in the snow. Adrenaline drove him to remove his own coat as well, thinking the extra warmth could make a difference for Chip. His shoulder screamed in protest. Everything going black.

Where was the rest of his unit? What time was it? For that matter, what day was it?

Jonas slapped his hand over his left breast pocket for his pocket New Testament and a letter from Gracie that he always kept close to his heart. That New Testament had just been another military-issued item when he shipped off to Europe. But in the year and half since his parents died, it had become a lifeline.

He scooted toward the opening of the dugout and pulled back the flap. Sunrise. He felt behind him with his good arm and made contact with a flashlight. It, combined with the bit of morning sun, provided enough light for him to make out the form beside him. "Chip?"

No response. In his heart, Jonas knew the reason for his friend's silence.

"Oh, Chip. I'm so sorry." He would have to get word to Chip's wife. His little boy would grow up without his father.

Jonas tucked his overcoat around Chip's arms. A cloud from warm breath hitting cold air billowed in front of his face. His teeth chattered. Once again, he tried to fight off the chill with the army blanket, only to have his right arm make the process impossible.

How long had he and Chip been in the dugout? An hour? A day? The flashlight beam hit where he would have expected to see the chain of Chip's dog tags, but they were missing.

He listened for the sounds of battle he'd grown so accustomed to, but even outside the shelter of the snow dugout, it was quiet. There was no telling how long that would last.

I have to get out of here. I have to find my unit. *He saw Gracie's face, smiling at him through her tears.* I need to get to Gracie. I promised I would come home.

Every move made Jonas's head pound. His shoulder screamed at him to find something to immobilize it. He could use the blanket to create a sling.

Chip—his friend who'd stood by him after he got news of his parents' death—lay so still, making his heart ache. Jonas gritted his teeth again and reached for his overcoat.

A rustling sound outside made him stop. Who was there? Was it an animal? Someone from his unit?

An enemy soldier?

Jonas gave himself permission to take a breath before ducking out of the dugout with only the blanket. He forced his body as far away from the scene as his legs would carry him.

Jonas kept hold of his arm, willing himself not to cry out and draw attention to his whereabouts. He stumbled in the snow for what seemed like forever, until the fog and pain in his head sent him to his knees and to the ground.

The feeling of being lifted roused him from sleep. He tried to say, "Let me go."

A voice shushed him before unconsciousness claimed him once more.

CHAPTER THIRTEEN

*L*aney took the rubber band off the large manila envelope and let it drop onto Janet's kitchen table. "It is so strange how a discovery like this can make other events clear for the first time."

"Like what?" Janet asked as she bustled around the room.

Laney sank into a chair at the table. "Grandpa Abe used to take road trips every year or so, always on a weekend, and leave Grandma at home. Sometimes she came to our house for a visit while he was gone. Sometimes, I happened to be at their house while my parents were out of town. I remember asking Grandma once or twice what Grandpa was doing, and she always said the same thing. 'Your grandpa's having some alone time.' Then we'd bake cookies, or she'd let me play dress-up with her old clothes, and I put Grandpa's absence out of my mind." Laney opened the envelope and let the cards and letters inside it pour over the table like rain. "Until now."

Janet carried two cups of coffee and a plate of molasses cookies to the table. The thing that stood out to her in the pile of letters were the international stamps. She checked a postmark. "These letters came from Belgium."

Laney picked up one of the letters. "This one is dated 1947." She pointed to the address. "It's addressed to a PO Box in St. Louis."

Janet picked up another letter. "This one is too." She sat with a handful of envelopes and spread them out like cards.

Laney held a letter in one hand and a postcard in the other. "A couple of these are addressed to Jonas Townsend." She let them fall onto the table. "I don't even know where to start reading."

Janet read the return addresses on a few of the envelopes. *DeSmett.* "How about if I help you put the letters in order of the date stamped on the envelope? It makes the most sense to me to read them in chronological order."

Laney took a sip of her coffee. "That would be great." Her phone dinged from inside her tote bag on the back of her chair. She dug it out to check it. "Reading these letters might need to wait. My car is ready."

"Wonderful. I'll take you over to get it."

After another quick sip of coffee, Laney returned the mail to its envelope. "I'd love to have your help another day, though. I think I'm going to drive home to Lakewood tomorrow and see if I can find anything else in Grandpa's files. Can we plan for the day after tomorrow?"

"Sure. We can have a letter-reading party."

"Invite your friend Debbie to join us. Might as well make it fun." Laney laughed and swung her tote over her shoulder. "What are we going to do about the letter that's in French?"

"We can try a translation app, but they're not always a hundred percent accurate. Maybe I'll get a lead on a translator while you're gone." Although she had no idea how she would manage that.

Laney dug through her tote. "Do you want to take pictures of the letter and the notes on the drawings?"

"I have a copier in the den." Janet led the way to it then carefully took the papers from Laney and began to run them through the machine.

"It's hitting me that Grandpa had a whole other life that none of us knew about," Laney observed as she watched. "Every return address I've seen so far had the surname DeSmett, but I don't remember either of my grandparents mentioning that name, or that they had friends in Belgium."

Janet watched the copier light sweep across the tray. "If Jonas Townsend fought in the Battle of the Bulge, it would make sense for him to have made a friend in Belgium. But he didn't survive the war, and that wouldn't explain your grandfather's connection. Something tells me that we're just starting to scratch the surface of this whole thing."

When Debbie came into the kitchen the next morning, Janet dropped her whisk into the bowl of pancake batter she was making and blurted, "Are you free tomorrow afternoon?"

Debbie set down her purse. "Good morning to you too. I think so." She pulled out her phone. "Nothing's on the calendar. What do you need?"

While Debbie grabbed an apron, Janet told her all about the safe-deposit box, the stack of letters, and the dog tags and documents bearing Jonas Townsend's name. "Laney and I were wondering if you'd be willing to go through all of that with us."

Debbie was so transfixed by her friend's words that she still held the apron, staring at Janet. Then she seemed to remember where she was and tied it into place. "I'm sorry. I'm trying to make sense of what you told me."

"I get it. Imagine how Laney feels. She's going home today hoping to find more information. So can you help tomorrow?"

"It's a date." Debbie went into the pantry and returned with a bottle of maple syrup.

Janet finished mixing the batter then tapped the whisk on the side of the bowl. "You didn't happen to take any French classes while living in Cleveland, did you?"

"French classes? No." Debbie set down the syrup and reached under the counter for the smaller syrup pitchers they put on the tables. "I did sign up for conversational Italian at the Cleveland Community Center when some ladies in my book club invited me to Italy with them. But the trip ended up being way too expensive for my budget, so I dropped the workshop. Why are you asking about French?"

"One of the letters that Laney found begins in English then changes to French."

"I can ask around." Debbie starting pouring syrup into the pitchers. "And maybe Patricia knows someone."

"I'll ask her when she comes in."

But by lunchtime, Janet was no closer to finding a local to translate Laney's letter.

She picked up a rack of clean water glasses and used her hip to open the kitchen door.

"Hi, Mrs. Shaw." Bethany Nickles stood at the counter with two other girls, her strawberry-blond hair free of its usual ponytail.

"Hello, Bethany. What are you doing out of school?"

"We have a short day because of teacher training. For honors history, we get extra credit if we go to a museum and write a summary of what we learn, so we went to the museum here at the depot."

"Good for you girls, doing something educational with your free time. I would've gone to a movie, so you're way more mature than I was at your age." Janet set down the glasses. "Are you here to claim your free cookie?"

Bethany peered into the bakery case. "Yeah. My friends are going to buy one as well."

"Great. What can I get for you?"

"Chocolate chip, please."

Her friends ordered the same.

"Coming right up." While opening the case, Janet glanced at Bethany, impressed by the girl. She took notes during club meetings, did extra credit on half days, and took honors classes. And the friends who'd accompanied her to the museum were either excellent students themselves, or at least cared enough about her to support her academic goals. "Hey, Bethany, I have a question for you."

"Sure, what do you need?"

"Do you happen to know anyone who speaks French?"

Bethany's two friends pointed to her at the same time and laughed at each other.

"Yes. Me," Bethany admitted, flushing.

One of the other girls nudged her. "Bethany's a genius. We hang out with her hoping some of her brains will transfer to us."

Bethany nudged her back. "That's not true. You're as smart as I am. We're in the same classes." She looked at Janet. "When I was ten, my family spent a summer in France when Dad had to go for a work thing."

"If it's okay with your parents, would you be willing to help me translate a letter for a friend of mine? It's in French."

"Sure. I'll text my mom now." She laid her coupon on the counter and took her phone out of her pocket. "I might even be able to help you later today."

"That would be amazing." Janet pushed the coupon back to Bethany. "Keep this for another day. All of you girls are getting free cookies today. You've made my afternoon." She set three bagged cookies on the counter.

Bethany took the bags and handed them out to her friends. "Thanks, Mrs. Shaw."

"Yeah, thanks so much."

Bethany's phone dinged, and she scanned the screen. "Mom's fine with it. I can meet you at the library later. It's close to my house."

"Four o'clock?"

"Four is great. See you then."

Janet waved to the girls as they left the café, already biting into their cookies.

Debbie came to the counter with a lunch order. "I see you found a translation service."

"I sure did. Now I need to pray that the letter—any of the letters, really—will include something that helps Laney."

Janet checked on the chicken defrosting in her refrigerator at home then found a safe place in her purse for the photocopies of the French letter and drawings. *Please, God, let this contain something helpful.* She grabbed her keys and headed out.

She found Bethany waiting for her in the young adult section of the library, typing on a laptop. "Hi, Bethany."

"Oh, hey."

"Doing homework?" Janet pulled out the chair across from Bethany.

"I'm finishing my summary of what I learned at the museum today. Our teacher knows most of us have been to the local museums before, so we have to highlight something that stood out to us in a new way." She shut her laptop.

"That's a clever twist." Janet took the letter out of her bag and laid it on the table. "Were you able to find something new?"

"Yeah. I think it's cool that the women at the canteen brought food from home for the soldiers at a time when they had to ration and make things stretch. They had so little, but they shared it anyway. So I'm writing about that. It makes me want to be more generous."

"I've always found that moving too." Did Rodd know what an incredible granddaughter he had?

Bethany reached for the letter. "You ready to see what this says?"

"Definitely."

CHAPTER FOURTEEN

Southern Belgium
January 4, 1945

The cot creaked when Jonas stirred. The cozy weight of a duvet covered him in such warmth that he expected to open his eyes and see the walls of his bedroom in Dennison, even though his bed at home had a bedspread and smelled different than this one.

With his eyes still closed, he ran his hand over his arm and shoulder and discovered that someone had wrapped both in a thick bandage and sling. The wound on the back of his head still throbbed. He forced his eyes open. Someone had taken off his uniform shirt, leaving his undershirt on, and changed him into a pajama shirt with his wrapped arm out. The sheet covering the mattress felt damp, as did his clothing. It reminded him of when he had the flu as a kid and his fever finally broke in the middle of the night.

Jonas remembered being lifted from the snowy ground, and the homey warmth melted into dread. Until he considered the warm duvet and clean shirt. Nazis wouldn't treat him this well.

He stared at the bare light bulb on the ceiling over his head and shifted his eyes to survey the rest of the room. He seemed to be in a basement, tidy and quiet. A few jars of canned fruits and vegetables stood in neat rows on shelves that lined one wall.

He'd heard stories of Nazis taking up residence in civilian homes. But wouldn't an officer be at his bedside by now, barking at him in German?

Jonas eyed the small square table to the right of his bed. It had a cup of water on it, his Gideons New Testament with Gracie's letter still tucked inside, and a little vase with a child's drawing of flowers propped against it.

Flowers? I'm definitely not a prisoner.

Jonas sat up slowly and groaned. A well-loved stuffed rabbit peeked out from under his blanket. What in the world?

He heard whispers from the basement stairs. Children's voices, speaking French. Jonas rubbed the back of his head and shifted his body so he could lean against the brass headboard.

Two faces watched him from the stairs leading to the tiny basement room. A little boy, about four or five, and a girl, who appeared to be seven or eight.

The little girl sprang up, her messy brown braids dangling over her shoulders, and shouted up the stairs, "Maman!"

The boy kept his big blue eyes fixed on Jonas.

Jonas gave him a little wave.

The boy waved his fingers in return. He took hold of two of the wooden rails and pressed his face against them with a goofy grin that made Jonas chuckle.

The door at the top of the stairs opened. The little girl pointed to Jonas.

He recognized her French word for "awake" and the gist of her mother's response. It sounded like she would be down in a moment.

The fog in his brain started to clear. He vaguely recalled tossing and turning on the cot, a woman with a basin, a cool cloth on his forehead, his own voice mumbling, "Mom, my arm hurts. Tell Gracie I'm sorry I can't make it tonight." Voices murmuring what sounded like prayers around him. A little girl singing a lullaby in French and rubbing his head. A small hand patting his shoulder. Larger hands lifting his head and placing something under it. Dreams about Chip trying to feed him franks and beans with a dry biscuit instead of a spoon.

He managed to smile, attempting to put the children on the stairs at ease. "Bonjour."

The girl said, "Bonjour."

The boy kept staring until his sister nudged him and he mumbled, "Bonjour."

Jonas pointed to the flower drawing then at the children. "From you?"

The girl smiled and nodded.

"Merci." Jonas expected to see his high school French teacher pop out of nowhere and correct him for his American accent. "Monsieur Townsend, you don't want to sound like an American tourist."

He tried to remember as many French phrases as possible.

Le livre est sur la table. *The book is on the table.*

Je voudrais un café et un croissant, s'il vous plait. *I would like a coffee and a croissant, please.*

Why couldn't he remember anything more useful?

He examined the sling around his bandaged arm. It was made of gingham, as if the woman upstairs had used a scarf or some fabric intended for a dress. On his pillow, he saw a damp rag and guessed it was a compress for the goose egg on his head. It smelled of herbs that he couldn't name.

A slender young man around Jonas's age stepped around the boy and girl, carrying a wooden crate. He said something in French that made them both laugh. When he reached the bottom of the stairs, his limp told Jonas why he was home instead of fighting the Nazis. The strength of his arms showed through his thin shirt and threadbare sweater. He set the crate in the corner beside a box of kindling but never took his gaze off Jonas.

He came over to the foot of Jonas's bed. "You are better?"

Jonas made another attempt to move his shoulder and grimaced. His body felt far from okay. But he was alive, and in a home rather than a Nazi bunker, so he nodded.

The young man pointed to Jonas's shoulder. "Dislocated. And shrapnel."

That explained the pain.

Seeing the concern in the man's eyes, Jonas once again remembered the feeling of being lifted off the ground. It must have been him. He held out his unbound hand. "Jonas."

The young man shook the offered hand. "Jean."

A woman with a long dark braid hanging down her back descended the stairs with a tray. Jonas knew her kind face. The woman with the basin. He'd called her "Mom" in his sleep.

She said something to the children, and they hopped up to follow her. The little girl moved the vase and picture from Jonas's bedside table to another small wooden table under the stairs, taking care to make sure Jonas could still see it.

The woman motioned for Jonas to sit up straighter, and set the tray in his lap. It held some kind of soup and a slice of dark bread. Then she put her hand on Jonas's forehead and cheek and smiled.

Jean said, "No more fever." He told the kids, "God answered your prayers."

The little girl clapped her hands and beamed, her eyes sparkling.

Jonas let the fragrance of the food fill his nostrils then reached for the spoon with his left hand. "Merci." His stomach responded to the meal with a loud growl. How long had it been since he ate? The water glass was almost empty, so he must have drunk.

The woman stepped back. "Tu parles Français?"

"Yes. I mean, oui." He bobbed his hand from side to side to indicate that his French was so-so then did his best to explain that he'd studied French in high school. "Tu parles Anglaise?"

"A little." The woman gave him a shy smile. She pointed to Jean. *"He is better with English. Teaching me."*

Jonas managed a spoonful of soup with his non-dominant hand and found the broth surprisingly flavorful despite the lack of meat. He told himself to eat slowly—that his stomach wasn't ready for much even though he felt famished—and tried to ignore the discomfort of eating with four sets of eyes watching him. He wiped his mouth and introduced himself to the woman. *"I am Jonas."*

"I am Edda," the woman told him. She went over to the children and placed her hand on top of the girl's head. *"Mila."* Then she put her arm around the little boy with the huge blue eyes. *"Oskar."* She acknowledged the older son, Jean, whom Jonas had already met.

For the next half hour, through a combination of Jonas's mediocre French, Edda's limited English, and Jean's attempts at interpreting, Jonas learned that Jean had found him while collecting firewood in the forest almost a week before, and he had been in and out of consciousness since then. He had a dislocated shoulder, a deep shrapnel wound in his upper arm, and—based on what Edda had learned from her mother, who had been a nurse—a concussion. The shrapnel wound had gotten infected. He had a high fever when Jean *found him. At one point, the family thought he would die, so all of them had gathered around him to pray.*

The memories of those strange dreams made sense now.

Under any other circumstances, Jonas would want to know why they had kept him at home instead of taking him to a hospital. The fact that he was in the basement rather than an upstairs bedroom told him why. The Allies had liberated much of Belgium, beginning in September. He had no idea if his division's efforts had freed the Bastogne region where Chip died. But since he was relatively hidden, there must still be some kind of Nazi presence in this area. Having an American soldier in their home put this family in danger.

Unless they were some of those collaborating with the Nazis.

He froze for a moment then relaxed. The peace in the room told him he was in safe hands.

Jonas dipped his bread into the remains of the broth at the bottom of his bowl. "Merci, Jean. For saving me."

Jean patted his own leg, the one that caused his limp. "When I got this, another soldier saved me from being captured. So I helped you."

Jean shared that he had been wounded while fighting in the resistance against the Nazis. Edda didn't mention a husband. The sadness in her eyes revealed the reason for his absence before Mila did, quite matter-of-factly.

"Papa est avec Jésus." Papa is with Jesus.

Edda turned her face, but not before Jonas saw her tears. She blinked them away and pulled a rickety chair beside Jonas's cot. "Gracie. She is your chéri?*"*

Sweetheart. How did Edda know about Gracie? He must have talked about her while the fever raged. "Oui."

Edda explained in French that he had been asking for her. Then she asked about his parents.

A lump formed in Jonas's throat. "They, um…" He fought for control, swallowing hard. "They are also with Jesus. They died in an automobile accident."

"Oh." Edda's brown eyes filled with such compassion that Jonas almost lost his grip on his emotions. She put her hand on her heart and murmured, "Je suis désolé." Jonas could tell she truly was sorry for his loss, as she knew grief well herself.

Oskar came to Jonas's bedside. He took the stuffed rabbit out from under the damp blanket and set it closer to Jonas. He gave Jonas a sad smile and patted his arm.

Jonas chuckled. "Merci, Oskar."

Jonas was grateful for everything they'd done. He was still hungry, but he had already imposed so much on this little family that he couldn't bring himself to ask for more.

Jean went upstairs then returned with a fresh duvet cover and sheet, along with a change of clothes, worn but clean and neatly folded.

Edda took Jonas's tray and offered to fill a tub for him to bathe—as well as he could with his wounded arm.

Heaven knows I need it.

"Merci." He pushed back the quilt.

Edda explained that she would change his bed coverings while he bathed and changed.

His legs felt weak when he stood. The more he recalled and let the memories sink in, the more desperate he felt to find his unit. Gracie. He'd written a letter to her and left it in the pocket of his overcoat. He flashed back to the moment he'd crawled out of the dugout, leaving his coat behind as a covering for Chip.

He tried to tell Edda that after his bath, he must go. He had to find out where his unit was.

The woman put her hand firmly on his shoulder. "Non. Nazis. Not safe."

"But that's why I need to get back. We're helping the Allies to liberate you from the Nazis."

Nazi-occupied Belgium had strict censorship, so Edda, Jean, and the children might not know they were in the process of being freed.

Edda shook her head, her eyes wild with fear. "Not safe."

He tried again to explain, this time in French.

But even then, Edda was insistent. She patted his shoulder in a way that reminded him of his mother. "Stay. We keep you safe."

"Gracie. I need to write to her."

"Non."

Jonas didn't ask why. He knew. Nazis read and censored the mail in countries they occupied.

Jean finished for his mother. "The Nazis will know you are with us if you write."

Jonas realized he had to make a choice between staying and being safe—or doing the right thing and risking death.

CHAPTER FIFTEEN

"Aw," Bethany said. "This letter is so sweet."

"What does it say?"

"It says, 'Dear Jonas. It has been an honor to have you as our guest. I pray that your wounds heal fully and that our kind heavenly Father will help you in your grief for losing your dear parents and then your friend.'" Bethany frowned. "How sad."

"I know. He suffered so much loss in a short time."

Bethany raised her head. "I didn't even think to ask before I started reading. Do you want to record this or something?"

"Good idea." Janet fumbled through her tote bag for her phone and pulled up the voice memo app. "Go ahead."

"I'll start over." Bethany reread the first part of the letter. "Edda wrote, 'That first day when you woke up in our home, you must have thought I was trying to hold you captive.' Ooh, thanks for asking me to help with this. It's getting really intriguing now."

"It is indeed," Janet said.

Bethany flipped the sheet over and kept reading. "'Now that we are free, I am sure you understand that I was frightened because of the Germans. Caring for you in your time of need and making a new friend was worth it. You will always have a family here in Bastogne. If God provides the means for you to return one day, you are always welcome in our home. Please write and let us know when you reach America and your home in Ohio safely. I will continue working on my English and practice in letters to you. Make me practice more by writing in English, please. Kindest regards, Edda DeSmett.' Then there's a note at the bottom from someone named Jean, which is the French version of John. It's in English."

Janet put her elbows on the table. It was a beautiful letter, but it never mentioned Abe Halner. "I didn't notice the extra note at the bottom. What does it say?"

"It says, 'Until we meet again, and I beat *you* at chess for once. Safe travels, Jean.'" Bethany laughed again. "That is such a guy thing to say. So competitive."

"Evidence that people never change." Janet shut off the recorder.

"Nope. Just fashion and technology, and fashion comes back around every couple of decades or so."

Janet chuckled and said, "I saw that the letter was written in 1945, but I was so thrown off by the words being in French that I didn't check the rest of the date."

Bethany flipped back to the front of the letter. "May 13, 1945." She gave it back to Janet. "Who's Jonas?"

"Jonas Townsend lived in Dennison until he enlisted in World War II." Janet debated whether to tell Bethany about Jonas's KIA status and Laney's search for clues about her grandfather's possible connection to Dennison. She decided against going into too much detail, since Laney was still trying to connect the dots herself. "A friend is trying to learn more about her family and found that letter in a safe-deposit box. We thought it would be helpful to know what it says."

Bethany handed the letter back to Janet. "I hope the translation gives her some answers."

"We found some drawings with notes on them. Do you mind taking a look at my copies of those as well?"

"Not at all." Bethany covered a smile. "I'm such a nerd, getting all excited about pictures from eighty years ago."

"Nerds rule the world, my friend." Janet showed her the drawings. One showed a childish attempt at a tank with a smiling stick man standing on top of it. Another stick man stood in front of the tank. He had a frown on his face. Each figure had words over his head. "I can read the name over the head of the guy on the tank. It says 'Jonas.' But I don't have a clue about the rest. I'm sure all the words were printed by this child's mother."

Bethany took the picture and leaned her elbow on the table. She laughed. "It says, 'Thanks for helping us win the war. Oskar.' The words over the second figure are 'Bad man.'"

The other picture was signed *Mila*, a girl who was old enough to print neatly and draw detailed pictures. It showed a woman and a man holding hands. The man had his arm bound in a sling. Each figure had a voice bubble above their head.

Janet handed it over. "And here we have some vintage cartooning."

"This kid is a good artist. She wrote, 'Gracie, will you marry me?' And 'I will.'"

"How sweet." Janet set the pictures beside the letter from Edda. "Thank you, Bethany. You've gotten us a step closer to solving a very complicated puzzle." She glanced at the date again and gasped.

May 1945.

Ray had said Jonas was killed in the Battle of the Bulge, which had lasted from mid-December 1944 through January 1945. How could Edda and her children have written notes to a man who had already died?

Unless he hadn't.

The next morning, Janet had just enough time before the café opened to share the contents of the letter and her revelation with Debbie. "Jonas Townsend wasn't killed. At least, not when he was thought to have been."

"Could he have died after staying with the woman who gave him that letter?"

"I guess it's possible, but what about Abe?" Janet slid a tray of mini pumpkin-chocolate chip muffins into the oven. The customers loved them.

"Janet, I just thought of a possibility. You said the letter mentions Jonas losing one of his friends."

"Yeah." She set the timer for fifteen minutes, guessing what Debbie would say.

"If Jonas was reported killed in action and Laney found his belongings in her grandfather's safe-deposit box, could Abe have spent some time during the war pretending to be Jonas?"

"Oh dear. What an awful thought." But it was a possible explanation.

Janet spent the rest of the morning mentally preparing for how Laney might feel when she heard the translation and possibly came to the same conclusion.

When Harry and Crosby came in for breakfast along with Ray, thanks to a Good Shepherd assistant, Janet wanted to tell them about the letter. But she decided Laney should hear those things first.

So she chatted with Ray and Harry about the baking contest while Debbie took their order for coffee and the morning's special, blueberry pancakes. She decided to deliver the order herself, and when she did, she found them drinking their coffee and talking about Jonas.

"Which division was he in again?" Harry asked.

"The Tenth Armored Division, called the 'Tiger Division.' That's what I heard when I returned to Dennison."

Janet set their plates in front of them. Would Laney come back to Dennison with new information? Perhaps something that made Janet's thoughts about the letter less surprising?

Harry pinched off a piece of his pancake and fed it to Crosby. "Everything okay, Janet?"

"Yes. I'm fine. It's just interesting that Jonas's name comes up in so many conversations these days."

Ray spread butter on his pancakes. "I've been thinking about Jonas a lot lately. With his parents gone, he never got a proper funeral that I know of. I'm not even sure where he's buried."

"That's so sad," Janet said.

"It is. I never felt as if I got the closure I needed to grieve him properly and begin to heal. It was so bad that I almost didn't believe he was dead. Once, after the war, I even thought I saw him."

Janet froze. "Really?"

Ray drizzled syrup over his breakfast. "It was a few weeks after I returned to Dennison. One morning I woke up early and couldn't get back to sleep. It happened a lot then. I went for a walk to clear my head and ended up on the street where Jonas had lived."

Janet supposed that was normal, since Ray and Jonas had been so close growing up.

"I saw a man walking away from the Townsend house, carrying a suitcase and wearing a letterman sweater identical to the one Jonas wore during our senior year of high school. He'd earned a letter for track. Lots of guys had the same sweater, but something about the man's walk reminded me so much of Jonas that I even called his name. Of course, he kept walking without so much as a pause in his step. I had to sit down on a bench to get ahold of myself. I felt like I'd seen a ghost. 'What are you thinking?' I asked myself. 'That wasn't Jonas. He died in the Battle of the Bulge.'"

Janet wasn't so sure, but it wasn't the time to say so. Not until she'd spoken to Laney.

Ray forked up a bite of pancake and let it hover over his plate. "At the time, every other man I saw reminded me of one who didn't come home. That poor man probably thought I'd lost my mind. Maybe I had. Temporarily anyway."

Janet stood silent. Debbie poured coffee for a couple at the next table, but Janet could tell from the tension in her friend's shoulders that she was listening to their conversation.

Harry added a little more sweetener to his coffee. "Well, if you'd lost your mind, so had I. Because I thought I saw Jonas once too, right here at the train station. It was also after the war, but late at night when soldiers were coming home. I finished a shift later than usual and saw a man who was the spitting image of Jonas getting off a train with a bunch of other servicemen. It spooked me so much that I had to step inside the waiting area until my heart stopped racing. Eileen had left for the night, so I couldn't tell her what happened. I remember telling another friend about it the next morning, and having a long talk about how strange it felt that the war was finally over, but things would never be the same."

The need to prepare another customer's order drew Janet back to the kitchen. By the time she came out with the breakfast order, Harry and Ray were almost finished eating.

Debbie whisked the order out of Janet's hands, so Janet grabbed the coffeepot and replenished Ray's half-empty mug. "So, Ray, did Harry tell you about the baking contest?"

"He sure did. Count me in. Eileen asked me to pass on her agreement as well."

Debbie handed Janet another table's breakfast order. Janet hurried back to the kitchen, where her thoughts shifted to Jonas, who'd never had a funeral, and Abe Halner who had Jonas's identification hidden away.

Laney called around midmorning. "Hi, Janet. I'm on my way to Dennison right now. You won't believe what I found at Grandpa's house, under his bed."

Her tone brought Janet some relief. She didn't sound upset. "What?"

"More letters from Edda DeSmett and some other people with the same last name. I wonder why he put some in the safe-deposit box and kept the rest at home."

Janet took a refill container of ranch dressing out of the refrigerator and set it beside the salad fixings. "Hopefully we can figure that out. I got your letter and pictures translated by a very smart thirteen-year-old from the Culinary Art Club."

"Fabulous. Are you and Debbie still available to sort through everything?"

"We sure are. Meet us at my house at three thirty this afternoon."

Janet set a vase of daisies she had bought at the store on the way home in the center of her dining room table.

She fluffed the flowers and spoke to her cat, who watched her from the doorway. "I know what you're thinking, Ranger. That this is an organizing get-together, not a party. But when you get a trio of women together, flowers are always called for."

She placed the phone with the recording of Bethany's English translation on the table. "Lord, we need to know what Abe was doing with Jonas's things, and what that has to do with a picture of the Townsend house."

When the doorbell rang, Janet's Yorkshire terrier, Laddie, barked like the Great Dane he thought he was. Janet scooped him up and carried him to the door. "Be polite, or you'll get banished to the back bedroom, and that will make you feel sad and left out."

Laney stood on her porch with a shoebox in her hands and a tote bag hanging from her arm. "Hello. Who is this little guy?"

Janet laughed while her dog wiggled so hard at his new friend that she nearly dropped him. "This is Laddie, our guard dog."

Laney tucked the box under her arm and held her hand out to Laddie before rubbing his head. "Hi, Laddie. You sure are a cutie."

Janet set Laddie down and held the door open for Laney. "If he gets to be too much, let me know."

"He's fine. We had a Yorkie when the girls were little."

"Debbie should be here any minute. Can I offer you some tea or coffee?"

"Tea would be great." Laney followed Janet into the kitchen and put her shoebox on the counter. "Did the letter contain anything interesting?"

Janet turned on the electric kettle. "Yes, it did. In fact, maybe you can listen to the recording while the water boils." She showed Laney to the place she'd set up in the dining room.

"That sounds great. Thank you."

Janet opened the recording app for Laney then found a paper she'd used to write the translations of the kids' notes. "Be sure to read the English translations of the drawings. It will double the cuteness factor."

Laney tapped the play button on Janet's phone and started listening. Janet went to the kitchen to fill two mugs and get one down for Debbie. She grabbed a selection of tea bags out of the cupboard and put them in a bowl.

When she returned to the dining room, Laney had her reading glasses on and the children's pictures spread out in front of her, along with the translation of their notes. She smiled at Janet. "These pictures are priceless."

"Aren't they?"

"But the letter from this woman, Edda, confuses me. It's written to Jonas near the end of the war. It's clear that Jonas stayed with Edda and her family for a time and that he had some kind of injury. But your friend Ray said Jonas died in the Battle of the Bulge, didn't he?"

"I know. The dates don't line up. But maybe the other letters will reveal more."

Laney moved Janet's phone to the middle of the table. "It's obvious that Jonas lost a friend, I assume in the war, but since Edda didn't mention the friend's name, I don't know who she means. So did my grandfather enter the scene before Jonas died or after?"

Janet could feel Laney's deepening confusion from across the table and wished she could shed any light on the situation. "Your guess is as good as mine. I was hoping that our time together today might reveal something."

Laney took the lid off the shoebox she'd brought. The sight of even more letters made the task ahead feel more daunting, even though something in the box might offer the answers they longed for. One detail offered a bit of relief. Rather than a stack of mail that had been tossed into the box over time, the letters and cards were neatly lined up on their sides.

"Maybe the notes from Edda and her family will make more sense after we read the others," Janet suggested. "If the mail in this box is as organized as it appears, it's probably in order by date. So first, we'll do the same with the letters you found last week and start from there. I'm sure I can find another shoebox to sort them into."

The doorbell rang when Janet was in the back bedroom, followed shortly by Laddie's bark.

Laney called, "You want me to get that?"

"Yes, please. It'll be Debbie." Janet found a box on the top shelf of the closet with an old pair of sandals in it. She moved the shoes to the shelf and hurried back to the dining room. "Found one."

When she reached the dining room, Laney held Laddie, and Debbie stood at the head of the table with to-go bags in her hands.

She set them on the table. "I brought snacks."

The aroma of french fries permeated the air. Janet inhaled deeply. "Good call, Debbie. And unhealthy snacks too, I smell."

Debbie pulled a cardboard to-go container out of one of the bags. "It'll be like a college all-nighter. I got a few different options."

Janet went to the kitchen for plates. "Ian is working a late shift tonight, so we have all the time in the world and won't need to worry about dinner now. Unless we want to add a healthy option later."

Laney set Laddie on the floor and took the plates from Janet. "I'm not usually one to stress-eat, but today I might make an exception."

Debbie unpacked the bags. "What did I miss so far?"

Janet caught her up. "We were about to put the letters in order."

They played the recording of the letter translation and started unpacking Laney's tote bag, which held the rest of the treasures they'd found in the safe-deposit box. Already the table reminded Janet of when Tiffany had brought friends over to work on group projects.

To protect the letters as they worked, Janet moved the snacks to the kitchen then grabbed a few plastic containers and brought them to the dining room. She lined them along one end of the table. "These will protect everything from potential drips or spills. One for the New Testament and letter, one for Jonas's identification documents and tags, and one for miscellaneous items. I have more if we need them."

"Perfect." Debbie moved her purse to the corner of the dining room. "What do you say we all get some food and get started?"

Laney dropped her empty tote bag beside Debbie's purse. "Sounds good."

Laddie followed Laney while she put a little of each snack on her plate. He whimpered.

"Don't fall for it, Laney. No matter how he behaves, he has eaten today, and we aren't so heartless that we never give him anything fun."

Laney chuckled. "Oh, I know. Our Yorkie tried to pull the same routine."

Janet was the last one to arrive in the dining room with her plate of fries, two pigs in a blanket, and two muffins. Laney had already distributed the items from the safe-deposit box into bins and emptied the folder of letters in the center of the table.

Laney took a step back. "Why do I feel like this pile of letters has grown since Monday? Not that there are nearly as many here as in the shoebox."

Janet patted Laney's arm. "Because the pile knows we're searching for answers. It can probably smell fear."

Laney laughed.

Debbie picked up a few letters and shuffled them around as she read the postmarks. "Hey, Laney, I found an envelope that has Jonas Townsend's name on it but no address. Should I put it in the miscellaneous bin or someplace else?"

"Go ahead and set it beside the miscellaneous bin for now, in case we find others like it."

Janet took a stack of three letters and sorted them into the shoebox she'd contributed alongside the ones Debbie had already arranged. Within a few minutes, all the letters from the envelope were in order except two.

Janet checked for postmarks. Neither had one.

Laney flipped through the row of letters with her fingertips. "All of these were written to my grandfather, except one addressed to Jonas Townsend. Most are from Edda DeSmett, except for a couple from Jean DeSmett and three from Mila and Oskar DeSmett."

"These are to Edda from Jonas Townsend," Janet said, showing them the envelopes she held, "but they don't have stamps, so he must not have been able to mail them."

Laney sat in her chair. "Are they sealed?"

"One is, the other isn't."

"Go ahead and check for dates on the letters themselves."

Janet lifted the flap on the unsealed envelope and pulled out the folded sheet. "May 18, 1945."

"And the other one?"

Janet carefully tore the envelope open. "May 15, 1945." She laid them both on the table.

Debbie finished off her fries. "So Jonas Townsend not only lived past the date when he is listed as killed in action, but he survived the war." She wiped her fingers on a napkin and picked up the letters. She put her hand over her mouth for a moment. "Janet, did you see the return address on these?"

"Not yet. I was so focused on Jonas's name that my eyes skipped it."

Debbie rotated both envelopes so she could see them. "They both say Dennison."

"Wh—" Laney took the envelopes from Debbie and read them. "I know this address."

"You would know it too," Debbie told Janet. "It's the address for the Townsend house."

CHAPTER SIXTEEN

*L*aney's phone pinged, breaking the stunned silence that had fallen. "Let me check that in case it's Brian." She reached for her purse. "It's my mom. Do you mind if I take this in the kitchen?"

"Wherever you want." Janet sat beside Debbie and dipped a fry into some ranch dressing. She heard the door to the backyard open and shut.

Debbie went to the kitchen and came back with a glass of water. "Do you think Jonas and Abe might be the same person?"

Janet bit into her french fry. "But Jonas was listed as killed in action."

To confirm what she'd been told once and for all, Janet picked up her phone and typed Jonas's name and hometown into her browser. One of the first results she clicked on was an image of a list of fallen servicemen from January 1945. "His name is right here."

The back door opened and closed again. Laney came into the dining room and dropped her phone into her purse. She collapsed into her chair then reached for her mug of tea, which must have cooled to room temperature.

"Want a warm-up?" Janet asked.

Laney shook her head. "Maybe later. I need a moment after what Mom just told me. Not that I'm all that shocked now."

Debbie broke one of her muffins in half. "What did your mom have to say?"

"My mom is Grandpa Abe's oldest daughter, and she's been dealing with all the paperwork since his death, including requesting copies of Grandpa's death certificate."

"That's never easy," Janet murmured.

"According to the person she talked to at the Department of Health, the name Abraham Halner came up as an alias or name change."

Debbie coughed, obviously as startled as Janet was.

"Mom ordered copies of the certificate anyway. The woman will include information on how to amend the certificate to reflect Grandpa's previous identity in case the family wants to do that. Of course, Mom was extremely confused. I hadn't told her what I found in the safe-deposit box because I wanted to wait until I had the full scoop. So I told her I found some things that indicated he might have changed his name at some point, but I don't know when or why. I promised to fill her in when I know more." Laney drank some of her tea. "Mom is upset. She's afraid we might find out someone stole her dad's identity. I told her not to jump to conclusions—that people change their name for lots of reasons."

Janet dunked a fry into the ketchup cup on her plate. "I researched Jonas's name, and he is definitely listed as killed in action."

Laney wrapped both hands around her mug. "What if Grandpa changed his name because he did something wrong? He didn't seem like that kind of person, but how would I have been able to tell if he was?"

Janet scooted her chair closer to Laney. "We haven't read any of the other letters yet, so there is still a lot we don't know. Like you told your mom, let's not jump to conclusions."

Laney glanced at the box they'd filled with letters. "You're right. This is about finding the truth, no matter what that is, and there is only one way to find out."

Janet patted the table. "I agree. Where would you like to start?"

"Maybe with the V-mail letter inside the New Testament. My guess is that if it's saved in a Bible, it must be special."

Debbie came over and put her hand on Laney's shoulder. "And whatever we discover, we are right here to support you."

"That's right." Janet patted Laney's hand. "You're with friends."

Laney pulled the bin toward her. "Thank you."

She took out the New Testament and the letter and set them down, side by side. Laney put on her reading glasses and opened the miniature New Testament. The brown cover was worn and faded. Laney thumbed through the pages. "I see some verses and scriptures marked with brackets." She smirked. "Maybe we'll discover that it's a secret code or something."

Janet and Debbie sat quietly while Laney scanned the tissue-thin pages then set the Bible aside for the piece of V-mail.

"It's dated October 1, 1943. 'Dear Jonas. I think of you every moment and so wish I could be with you to comfort you as you grieve the loss of your parents. Since I can't be, here is my prayer for you.'" Laney stopped to adjust her glasses. "'Dear Heavenly Father, please be very close to Jonas. Surround him with Your angels of protection and surround him with Your love and comfort. Send him home safely to me. Amen.' Then she wrote the reference for Psalm 23."

Janet realized that she was starting to feel teary. "That's such a sweet letter." She sniffed, much to her own embarrassment. "I'm sorry. Clearly, I'm getting emotionally invested in this story."

Debbie picked up the pocket-size Bible and looked through it. "Psalm 23 is marked with a star and 'From Gracie.'" She handed it back to Laney. "Today I checked online when I had a little free time, and I learned that Larry and Bridget Townsend died on September 4."

Laney opened the New Testament. "He marked Psalm 25 too. That was one of Grandpa Abe's favorites. He also liked Job. I remember because, as a kid, that struck me as a strange book of the Bible to have as a favorite."

"I felt the same way then. I get it now, though. Let me refresh your tea," Janet offered. When Laney and Debbie agreed, she took all three mugs into the kitchen, dumped out the old tea, and then filled the mugs with fresh hot water.

Laney chose a peppermint tea and set it to steep. "After a letter like that, I would expect to see a pile of letters from Gracie, not a woman named Edda."

Janet tore open an orange spice tea bag. "Unless Gracie's letters ended up somewhere else. If Jonas was reported killed in action, the military would have sent all his belongings back to his family. I assume that would include any letters he'd saved. Since he didn't have a family, who knows where those things ended up? Or how these items got separated."

Laney picked up one of the unsent letters from after the war. She took it out and started reading. "This is to Edda, Jean, Mila, and

Rumors Are Flying

Oskar, written while waiting for his train from New York to Dennison. 'I hope the postcard I sent arrived safely. I will write again soon. I cannot wait to tell Gracie about all of you and give her the beautiful bracelet you gave me for her.'" She set the letter aside. "That's one question answered. Edda gave Jonas the fleur-de-lis bracelet for Gracie."

Debbie picked up her empty plate. "But he clearly didn't give it to her, because it was in the safe-deposit box."

Janet finished the last of her fries and moved her plate aside. "How could Jonas have arrived in Dennison if everyone who knew him says he died?"

"Are we all done eating? If we clear the table, we'll have more room to spread out the letters if we want to," Debbie said.

"I can get it," Janet said. "You're a guest."

"I haven't been a guest in this house for years. You've fussed over us enough." Debbie quickly cleared the plates and leftovers from the table. As she reemerged from the kitchen, she said, "Janet, I just thought of something. Remember the stories Ray and Harry told us about thinking they saw Jonas in Dennison?"

"Oh, that's right." Janet told Laney what they'd shared. "Maybe they weren't seeing things, if we have confirmation that he was taking a train here."

Laney picked up the envelope that didn't have an address on it and started to read.

Janet moved the New Testament and V-mail to the center of the table. "If someone was posing as Jonas, I wonder if Gracie caught on. She knew the man she loved, and the person who returned after the war wasn't him. She would have known."

"Wouldn't she say something if that was the case? Go to the police or something?" Debbie asked.

"Good point." *At a standstill again.* "Besides, Ray and Harry also knew him well, and they passed off their experiences as seeing things."

Laney gasped. "Oh my goodness."

"What?" Janet asked.

"This note." Laney looked up. Her eyes glazed with disbelief. "The one that didn't have an address on the envelope?"

"What does it say?" Janet got up and stood behind Laney to read over her shoulder. The little she read sent a chill through her body. "Who would write such a thing?"

Laney's voice was tight. "Jonas had lost both his parents and was fighting overseas, and someone was cruel enough to send him this?"

Janet took the note out of Laney's hand and read the entire thing. "This is horrible." She handed the paper to Debbie.

Debbie read the note and shuddered. "There's no name. Just a threat, signed with the initials C.B. and a phone number." She laid the page on the table.

Janet went back to her place at the table. "Coward."

Laney snatched up the note and read it again.

"Do you want to stop for a while? We can go for a walk to get some air, and read the rest of the letters later."

"No." Laney dropped the note as if it were red hot. She took another out of the box. "I need to know what really happened to Jonas and what all this has to do with my grandfather. And I need to know now."

CHAPTER SEVENTEEN

New York City, New York
May 15, 1945

Jonas dropped his duffel bag at the foot of the twin bed and looked around his bedroom for the night. Outside, he heard the honks of car horns and the bustle of city life. Now that he was back on American soil, his weeks hidden in the DeSmetts' basement as a protected recuperating guest felt like something he'd dreamed up.

He'd spent that time wondering who, if anyone, had found Chip. Playing chess with Jean. Singing French songs and playing jacks with Mila and Oskar. Telling stories about Dennison, Ohio, his friend Ray Zink, happy memories of his parents, and of Gracie. Wishing he could write to her without putting the DeSmetts in danger. Comforting the family with stories of the progress his division had made. Speaking more French than English some days, except when Edda declared an English Only night so she could learn more of the language and have Jonas teach the children some words and phrases. Knowing his unit had no idea where to find him and probably feared he'd been captured.

Then came the day in early February when Edda walked to town hoping to find bread to purchase and returned in tears.

"We are liberated! Everyone is celebrating." The Nazis had been completely driven out of Belgium.

Jonas ran to the center of town with Edda, Jean, and the children, and danced and celebrated as if he were a citizen of Bastogne. Finally, he could write to Gracie.

He did all he could after that to help the DeSmetts' community recover from years of occupation. The end of the war had left Belgium in a different kind of crisis. They had the long task of rebuilding what the Nazis destroyed. All he'd been able to think about while serving the family that kept him alive was home and figuring out how to get there. He would kiss Gracie first and report to the army next.

But first, he needed money. So he'd done what he always did when he needed something his parents couldn't afford—he used whatever skills he had to earn *the funds. By the time he said goodbye to the DeSmetts, the war in Europe was over.*

As a veteran in civilian clothes, even the room in New York felt foreign. He sat at the foot of his bed. Thank You, God, for the kind ladies who offered me this room for free. *They'd insisted when they'd learned he was returning home after fighting in Europe. Lila and Bertha Grady had given him dinner, sent him up to his room with a paper bag full of popcorn to snack on later, and told him he would find stationery in the desk by the window if he wanted to write to someone.*

"There's a post office right down the street, on the way to the train station," Lila had added before he went upstairs for the night.

Jonas set the popcorn on the nightstand beside his bed. He massaged his right shoulder and reminded himself for the hundredth time what Edda told him before he left her home. Healing would take time, and he needed to be patient—with his shoulder and his grief. The smell of popcorn reminded him of sitting beside Gracie at the movies before he left for boot camp. They'd always shared popcorn. Gracie must be worried sick. *He'd written to her every week since the liberation and given her the DeSmetts' address to reply. But he'd never gotten one, which told him that either his letters had never reached her, or her replies hadn't reached him.*

"Because of the war," Edda insisted. "Everything's still a mess."

Now that he sat alone in a strange bedroom, Gracie's face was all he wanted to see.

Until he thought about his folks and pictured himself walking into the empty house that had once been home. "God, I wish I could jump ahead in time to when Gracie and I are married."

Gracie. If only he could call her and hear her voice. But New York to Dennison was long-distance, and he couldn't bring himself to take advantage of his hosts' kindness by asking to make such a call on their dime. He thought about Lila and Bertha's offer of stationery. By the time the letter arrived in her mailbox, he would be home. Home, where he could finally take her in his arms, give her a kiss, and tell her what a difference her letters had made for him.

Home, where he could finally get to the bottom of his parents' death.

Though he'd likely make it home before a letter, Jonas still wanted to write to Gracie now that he'd finally reached America. He set his duffel on the bed and unzipped the main compartment. He dug to the bottom until he found a square box.

For your Gracie.

The gold fleur-de-lis bracelet inside had belonged to Edda DeSmett's mother. He'd tried to refuse it. "I can't accept this."

Unfortunately, he'd already told her and the kids about his and Gracie's childish plan to pretend that he was going on an exotic trip to Paris with the French Club, and his naive promise to bring her back something pretty.

"No, no, Edda. That promise was a game to make us both feel better. I didn't tell you that story because I expected you to—"

But she hadn't let him finish. "Gracie has been sick with worry. I know how that feels. When Jean and his father went away to join the resistance, I could not sleep or eat. When you see Gracie again, I want you to be able to give her the something pretty you promised her. Mila will inherit my wedding pearls, Oskar will have his father's watch, and Jean his grandfather's gold ring. I have an emerald ring that belonged to my mother. This bracelet is for Gracie."

He sat at the end of the bed and opened the box. He tried to picture Gracie's face when he finally got to give it to her. God, how will I ever be able to thank Edda and Jean and the children properly for all they did for me? I wouldn't have survived the war without them.

Maybe he could start with a letter letting the family know he'd made it to New York. He went to the wooden desk by the window and opened the long narrow drawer. Inside was a stack of letter paper, some envelopes, two pencils, and a small stack of postcards clipped together with a note that read, Feel free to use.

Jonas smiled and unclipped the stack. A postcard from America would be perfect. Mila and Oskar would love it. One card had a picture of the Statue of Liberty, another the Brooklyn Bridge at sunset, and two featured Central Park. He chose the Statue of Liberty for the DeSmetts and the Brooklyn Bridge card for Gracie. He settled himself into the desk chair, feeling like a kid about to do his homework.

He wrote Gracie's card first.

Hey, Gracie, look where I am!

New York City!

By the time you get this, I'll be home, but this helps me feel as if I can talk to you already.

I miss you more than I can express.

All my love,

Jonas

He addressed the postcard and set it aside to mail.

For the sake of Edda's determination to learn English, he kept the letter to her family simple.

Bonjour, Edda, Jean, Mila, and Oskar!

I made it to New York City. Tomorrow, I leave for Dennison, Ohio.

Thank you for your kindness and hospitality.

I will always be grateful for you.

Your friend always,

Jonas

He went to his duffel to retrieve the DeSmetts' mailing address, added it to the postcard, and tucked both cards into his New Testament, behind his treasured letter from Gracie, where it wouldn't get creased or smeared. If he left right after breakfast in the morning, he would have plenty of time to take them to the post office where he could buy an overseas stamp before buying his ticket and boarding the train to Ohio.

With a yawn, he reached for his bag of popcorn and took out a handful. The sun was still out. He couldn't go to bed yet.

Jonas scanned the room for something to occupy himself. On a bookshelf against the wall, he found a set of encyclopedias, a dictionary, and a row of mysteries for kids. He and Ray used to read those books together. He pulled one of the mysteries off the shelf to read until he felt tired enough for sleep. Then he spotted a newspaper on top of the encyclopedias and took that to bed too.

Jonas arranged the pillows against the headboard, set the popcorn beside him, and opened the newspaper first. It was from January, but it would do for a short break. He read reviews of movies he hadn't seen, weather that was long gone, and updates on a war that was now, thankfully, a thing of the past. He spotted the obituary section, as well as a list of American servicemen who'd been killed in action, but stopped himself before he read it.

He set the paper aside for the mystery novel, longing for an escape from the sadness he'd already lived through. I don't need to volunteer to be sad. *What if he saw the name of one of his friends?*

Chip might be on the list.

He picked the newspaper up again. His hands started to tremble at the thought of other men. Those in his unit that he'd fought alongside until everything went dark, and he woke up in the snow dugout.

He opened the section full of names. If I see a familiar one, at least I'll know. I'll find out while in a private place. *He mentally retraced the days to when Chip was killed. What day was that again? Sometime at the end of December. He would certainly be on this list.*

All the names beginning with A through R were strangers to him. Chip's name wasn't there. He started on S's then on the T's.

One name made his heart leap up into his throat. He knocked over his bag of popcorn as he shot up straight, the kernels spilling onto the bedspread.

"No." *Jonas's hand flew to his mouth.* "It's a mistake. It has to be."

He read the name again and again, his breath shallow.

That name. It wasn't just similar. It was his name.

Right there in black typed letters from January.

Townsend, Lieutenant Jonas C.

Seeing his name shouldn't have shocked Jonas. He'd gotten separated from his unit at the end of December. The more time that passed after he woke up in Edda DeSmett's basement, the more scenarios he'd created in his mind for what the army might have reported.

But none of them had included him being listed as killed in action. Wouldn't it make more sense to list him as missing? After all, it wasn't as if they had found his body.

How many people read that list and think I'm dead? The chilling thought haunted Jonas as he cleaned up the spilled popcorn, tried to sleep, got up to pace the room for two hours, tossed and turned until dawn, and made his bed the next morning. While brushing his teeth, he felt through the front of his T-shirt three times to confirm that he hadn't lost his dog tags.

What part of his uniform had he left behind after the explosion that changed everything? His helmet had been missing when he woke up in the snow dugout outside Bastogne. But finding that wouldn't lead someone to believe he'd died.

Chip's missing dog tags.

Leaving his coat over Chip.

Escaping the dugout with only his army blanket.

The overcoat had his name written inside. So did the unsent letter to Gracie. He had also put his most recent letter from Gracie in one of the pockets.

"But I wrote to Gracie once Edda said it was safe to." Did his KIA status explain why he hadn't received a reply?

The fog that followed him out of the snow dugout on that morning in late December when Chip died hung over him again as he packed up to leave the boardinghouse. As he walked out of his room and down the hallway for breakfast, he ached to tell someone, "The army made a horrible mistake. They reported me KIA. But I'm alive. You can see me, right?" But the words wouldn't come. Not when he accepted his plate of sausage, eggs, and toast, nor when he thanked the Grady sisters for the room and the meals and the lunch they sent him out the door with.

In line at the post office, he pinched his arm to remind himself he was still a flesh-and-blood human. He said hello to strangers to hear his own voice and each man's or woman's response.

Jonas paid for his stamps, let the sourness of licking the overseas postage linger on his tongue, and kept his hand on the mailbox handle after dropping the DeSmetts' card in. He stared at his postcard to Gracie. The idea of mailing a cheery card to a woman who thought he was dead sent a chill through him.

He needed to clear up the mistake in person. He couldn't imagine what she'd already been through if she'd been receiving letters from someone who wasn't officially alive.

Jonas put the Brooklyn Bridge postcard in his pocket.

He wanted to write Edda another letter to tell her what happened. But he was still making sense of the mistake himself. It would be better to wait until he had the whole matter cleared up. By then, he might even see the humor in it. "Guess who's back from the dead!" Won't this be a story for the grandkids someday.

Grandkids.

Gracie.

He stopped abruptly in the middle of the sidewalk, and a woman behind him had to step around him.

Oh, Lord. Poor Gracie. *What must it have been like for her to get the news of his death? His desperation to get to her and tell her he was alive and mostly well almost sent Jonas running for the train station. But he still had an hour to kill after he purchased his train ticket, and standing on the platform waiting for the sound of the whistle would only make the time go more slowly.*

He found a newsstand and bought a paper and a pack of chewing gum. He wrote a letter to the DeSmetts to mail when he got home, telling them about his trip to the States and describing New York City—what they might like to see if they ever made it to America.

Finally, a distant whistle announced the arrival of his train, and Jonas found a place at the back of the car by the window. He took a nap to pass the time, ate his lunch, and planned for how to sort out the mistake of his KIA status with the army.

Whom had they notified as next of kin when his parents were already gone? With no one in Dennison to deliver a telegram to, Gracie would have read his name in the newspaper.

The train slowed to a stop. Jonas peered out the window expecting to see a train station. Instead, he saw trees on one side and rolling hills on the other.

"Sorry, folks." A porter walked the aisle. "We're stopped for a freight train. As soon as it passes, we'll be on our way again."

Come on. Jonas squeezed his eyes shut, wishing his need to get to the woman he loved could make the freight train move faster.

Jonas's train was several hours late to the Dennison station, thanks to another long delay for a repair. It had barely stopped when he grabbed his duffel off the storage rack over his seat and made a beeline for the exit.

Dennison had never looked more beautiful than it did after two years away. In the cool spring air outside at the station, WELCOME HOME signs flapped in the wind. Servicemen who still had a long way to go until they reached home headed toward the line for the Salvation Army Canteen, but Jonas had no need for doughnuts, sandwiches, or even a cup of coffee. He didn't stop in the depot to see if Harry Franklin or Eileen Turner happened to still be on duty. They were probably long gone, and as much as he wanted to see their faces and let them see his, to tell them the news they'd heard about him was incorrect, Gracie needed to see him first.

His shoulder ached from the long journey, but all he cared about was Gracie. Until he realized what time it was, and that breaking the news that he was alive would have to wait till morning. It would give him time to think. To plan how to tell her without scaring her half to death.

He walked past the Pikes' house, which was completely dark. He imagined the whole family asleep inside, relieved to have Gracie's brother home after a long war.

But the house appeared vacant altogether.

It just seems that way because it's late, *he told himself.*

Jonas peered up at Gracie's bedroom window. Soon after they started dating during their junior year, Jonas had tossed pebbles at that window, like he and Gracie had seen in a movie. He chose that time of night knowing Gracie was probably in bed but not quite asleep yet. After the third pebble hit, Gracie opened her window and leaned out, so cute with her hair up in curlers and no lipstick on.

"Gracie Pike," Jonas remembered calling to her, loudly enough for her to hear without waking everyone else in the house, "will you go to the prom with me?"

"What are you doing, Jonas? You're going to get us both in trouble." But Gracie was smiling as she said it.

Until Mr. Pike came outside in his robe and slippers and ordered Jonas off his lawn and his daughter "back to bed before the whole neighborhood sees you."

Before closing her window, Gracie said, "I'd love to go with you," and blew Jonas a kiss.

Mr. Pike shook his finger at Jonas that night. "If you want my answer to the prom question to be yes, I better not ever see you throwing rocks or anything else at one of my windows again."

"Yes, sir. I apologize. It'll never happen again."

But Jonas caught Mr. Pike's shoulders shaking with barely contained laughter on his way back inside.

At prom, Gracie had told Jonas she would never forget how he asked her. "It was so romantic. And did you see my father's face? He wasn't even angry."

If he were coming home under normal circumstances, he would be tempted to announce his return home by tossing pebbles at Gracie's window again for old times' sake. But he couldn't bring himself to be the ghost that woke her in the middle of the night.

The comforting notion of seeing Gracie in the morning, saving up for a ring and finally proposing for real, and then spending the rest of his days with her brought light to the sad reality of going home to a house that had been empty for almost two years. That comfort gave Jonas the courage to find the spare key his parents had always hidden under the WELCOME mat, open the front door to that big house full of memories, walk upstairs to his boyhood bedroom with only his flashlight for illumination, and spend the night there knowing his parents' bedroom was empty. His father's Ford was no longer in the garage, so the chances of him being able to find out what had gone wrong with the brakes were slim to none.

When Jonas woke up in the morning, he half-expected to smell bacon and coffee wafting through the heater vent. He would go to the kitchen to find his parents discussing the latest war news, or figuring out the last clue of a crossword puzzle, or talking in tense tones until Jonas walked in and Mom asked, "How did you sleep?"

Instead, the whole house was as quiet as the dugout in Belgium.

The thought of finally seeing Gracie pulled Jonas out of bed and into the bathroom for a bath and a shave by flashlight, but the water had been shut off along with the electricity after his parents died. He brushed his teeth as best he could, combed back his grown-out hair, and planned his speech, thankful for the gum he'd bought the day before.

"Gracie, it's me, Jonas. I know what you read in the paper. But it was a mistake. I'm alive. I tried to send letters, but—" She would throw her arms around him and insist on accompanying him to wherever he needed to go to report the mix-up to the army. He would give her the fleur-de-lis bracelet. On the way to straighten out the mistake, he would tell her all about the DeSmett family and about his friend Chip.

He dug through his duffel for the velvet box and slipped it into the pocket of his trousers. Then he checked his watch, and his shoulders slumped. It was barely after five in the morning. He blamed his early rise on his desperation to see Gracie.

He went to the kitchen to whip up some breakfast, only to find reminders that his parents hadn't been in the house to shop for food in a very long time, and he didn't have a way to cook anything anyway.

They really are gone.

Jonas shook off the urge to weep and went to the pantry in search of something that might have been left behind. The reality of his parents' absence weighed down his entire body. Someone—a neighbor perhaps— had been good enough to clear the refrigerator and bread box of food that would have spoiled ages ago. But they had left behind canned and dried goods in the pantry. Jonas found an unopened box of cornflakes and ate some dry from the box. I'll call the power company first thing after seeing Gracie.

How could he live in this house alone with the memories of his parents as his sole companions?

I won't be here alone for long. *As soon as he and Gracie married, they would live in it together. They would raise their children in the house. They had talked about their plans many times before he shipped off. They would have at least four kids because Jonas had always wished for siblings, a tree house in the backyard, and a porch swing out front.*

After the tragedy that took his parents, Jonas knew for sure that Gracie would insist on honoring them when it came time to choose names for their children. He tried to picture a baby Larry or little Bridget with his dark wavy hair and Gracie's blue eyes.

The longer he sat at the kitchen table thinking about his future with Gracie, the more anxious he felt to be with her. To let her know he was alive. To hug and kiss her and feel the sweet comfort of her gentle presence. To hear her laugh. To see her eyes sparkle when he gave her the bracelet.

Gracie would understand if he showed up at her house early. At least she would when she saw Jonas's face. He checked his watch again. Five thirty.

Tick, tick, tick. It came from his watch, not the grandfather clock in the living room. When he walked into that room and looked up at the clock, the hands were stuck at ten minutes to six, marking the time the clock had wound down and never been rewound.

Jonas went back to the kitchen, sank into his old chair, and put his head in his hands. He could hear Edda's gentle voice assuring him, "You will see them again, as I will see my Lars again."

Tears choked him. He needed to get out of this house. Take a walk or something. The quiet and his hunger made him feel sadder and lonelier for his parents. He got up and started toward the front door again. He could practically hear his mother's voice scolding in her lighthearted way, "Jonas Allan Townsend. Did you forget something?" *He hurried to push his chair back against the kitchen table.*

In the entry hall, while taking his jacket off the coat-tree, he spotted something lying on the mat in front of the front door. Probably an old piece of mail.

He picked up the envelope and tore it open. The letter was dated two weeks after his parents died.

Welcome home, Jonas.

Allow me to introduce myself. My name is unimportant, but you can call me C.B. My condolences on the untimely death of your parents. Unfortunately, your father died owing me quite a hefty sum of money. Please contact me ASAP to discuss payment of his debt of $7,900 plus 10% interest every thirty days from the date of this letter.

It would be a shame to see you return from the war only to suffer the same fate as your mother and father.

Sincerely,

C.B.

PS. If you are considering going to the police with this letter, you would be wise not to do that.

There was a phone number to call.

Jonas's entire body went cold. He glanced over his shoulder, expecting to see a shadowy man in a black hat and trench coat and hear a sinister voice introducing himself as C.B.

His first impulse was to hurry to the phone, dial the number at the end of the letter, and say, "I'll do whatever you want. Just tell me where to send the money." But he couldn't pay for any of it. Jonas's knees buckled. He sank onto the hallway bench beside the coat-tree and read the letter again. He tried to do the math for the original debt plus two years' worth of interest, and the numbers made his mind spin.

What was he going to do?

CHAPTER EIGHTEEN

Dennison, Ohio
May 16, 1945

The home that had once been Jonas's haven suddenly felt like a prison cell. If he went outside now, how long would it take before C.B. found him and demanded his money?

Jonas reread the postscript of the letter, which warned him against going to the police. Everything he'd been through over the past two years raced through his mind. He lifted his chin and squared his shoulders. "I survived a war. I'm not going to let this thug scare me away from turning him in."

I told you he couldn't be trusted.

It was just a card game.

But given this note, it had been much more than a card game.

Who was this C.B. person anyway? Jonas sprang to his feet and went to the one place where he had a chance of finding out. His father's study. As soon as he saw the desk that his father had been sitting at, his back to the door, when Jonas overheard the phone call that ended with, "Leave them out of this," and "Yes, I understand," he felt cold inside.

He pulled open the deep bottom drawer on the left side of the desk where his parents kept files for bills, the bank account, and every business that Dad had attempted. He saw one marked Loan, C. Baringer. *He pulled it out, sat in his father's chair, and opened the folder. The first page was a simple loan agreement. $2,500.* Purpose: Capital for Townsend Auto Repair.

The last business that his father had opened and quickly lost.

Other pages uncovered debts that made "Just a card game" a gross understatement.

"Dad, how could you do this?"

Because he was desperate to pay back the business loan and his creditor lured him into a deeper hole through gambling?

I'll never know. Except that this probably explains why Mom and Dad were driving on the interstate

WHISTLE STOP CAFÉ MYSTERIES

after midnight when the brakes failed. They must have been trying to get away from Dad's debts.

All of this could prove Jonas's conviction that the crash wasn't an accident.

Jonas shut the file, ready to take it and the letter to the Dennison Police Department.

Then the horrible realization hit.

Reporting the letter and the file folder would bring out his father's involvement in the card games he lost. The fact that he'd borrowed money from a bookie instead of a legitimate bank. The tragedy of his parents' death would be overshadowed by a shameful legacy.

What about Gracie? Did C.B. know about her? Jonas's inability to pay Dad's debt wouldn't only put him in danger. It might put Gracie at risk as well.

He sat rigid in his father's chair. In his mind, he saw the names listed as Killed in Action.

Townsend, Lieutenant Jonas C.

Whoever wrote the note would have seen that list at some point.

"Everyone thinks I died," Jonas whispered to the empty den. *The quiet of the big house made his voice echo.*

As long as C. Baringer went on thinking Jonas had been killed in Belgium, he would be safe.

Gracie would be safe.

We could elope and move. *Someplace far away. A smile spread over Jonas's face as he pictured putting his plan into action. Gracie might even think it sounded romantic to elope.* We could go to New York. She's always wanted to go there.

Then he realized that even an elopement would become public knowledge eventually. Gracie would tell her parents and her brother where they moved to. Her friends.

No matter where they went, he and Gracie would have an address that C. Baringer could eventually discover.

Jonas's hand grew sweaty around the file folder.

Unless they didn't tell anyone where they went.

He let his head rest against the wall behind Dad's chair.

It would be a shame to see you return from the war only to suffer the same fate as your mother and father.

A lump rose in his throat.

Oh, Lord, I love Gracie so much. She's all I have left. But can I really expect her to leave her home and spend the rest of her life on the run? I don't want her to have to live in fear because of me. *Tears filled* his eyes. *The idea of letting go of the woman he loved after losing Mom and Dad, Chip, and so many other friends felt like more than his heart could carry.*

He opened the file drawer and returned the folder to its place.

Gracie will be safer if she goes on thinking I died.

Jonas pulled his old suitcase off the top shelf of his bedroom closet. Carrying a duffel that resembled military gear would draw too much attention. He tossed in as many clothes and toiletries as he could fit in the suitcase he'd once used for camp and family vacations, along with everything he'd brought home from the war. He found room between his clothes for a few provisions from the pantry. He glanced at his watch. It was a quarter to seven. He needed to act fast to avoid being on the street when the rest of Dennison left their homes for work and school.

God, where should I go? *Taking the train was out of the question. Even if Harry and Eileen weren't working this early, he would see other familiar faces. He knew everyone who worked at Dennison Station. And everyone knew him. Jonas Townsend, who was killed in action in December 1944.*

Uhrichsville would be too risky as well.

The bus. *He could walk to the next town over from Uhrichsville and take a bus to the farthest city that his remaining dollars allowed with a little left over for food.*

Jonas searched every pocket in his closet, his nightstand, and his childhood piggy bank for spare change and found a total of seventy-three cents. He remembered his parents' emergency fund and prayed it was still inside the coffee can in their bedroom closet. He poured out a handful of change and thirty-five dollars in bills. Thank You, God. *It might not get him far, but it would get him somewhere.*

Jonas found his confirmation Bible in his nightstand drawer and his birth certificate and social security card in his desk from when he'd filled out his army paperwork. A leftover apple and oatmeal-raisin cookie from the last meal he'd bought while traveling home would have to tide him over until he could heat up one of the canned foods in his suitcase or buy a meal without being recognized. The next step after leaving town would be to change his name.

I don't even know how to do that. *He took a deep breath. One thing at a time. For now, he had to get out of Dennison before someone saw him and word got out that Jonas Townsend was alive.*

Five minutes later, Jonas locked the front door of the home he'd grown up in for the final time and returned the key to its spot under the mat. Dressed in jeans, his old high school letterman sweater for running track, and a baseball cap pulled down as far as possible, he hoped he'd achieved the anonymity he wanted. He patted the pocket where he'd stuck Gracie's postcard of the Brooklyn Bridge, determined not to leave anything in the house that linked him to her after December 1944. He would have to pray that his letters since then had been lost, or better yet, destroyed.

He walked as quickly as he could along the sidewalk without appearing to be on the run. He would have to stay clear of Gracie's house, Dennison Station, and Main Street and walk until he knew he could board a bus safely. However long that took. Don't stop for anything, *he told himself.* Keep your head down and your feet moving.

"Jonas?" The familiar voice called his name out of nowhere. "Jonas?"

Don't stop.

"Jonas, is that you? It's me, Ray Zink."

Jonas longed to stop. To tell Ray what happened as he always had. I'm in trouble, Ray. *But that might put his friend in danger.*

Keep walking.

"Jonas?" Ray sounded like he thought his eyes might be playing tricks on him.

Let him think he's imagining things. Jonas Townsend died in the war.

CHAPTER NINETEEN

Missouri
May 17, 1945

When Jonas saw the sign that said WELCOME TO MISSOURI, he finally gave himself permission to relax. He could be thankful for one thing besides being so many miles away from C. Baringer. In the hours since the bus had pulled out of Rockford, Ohio, no one had sat beside him. A stop for the driver to fuel up and passengers to stretch their legs had allowed Jonas to buy an inexpensive meal from a stranger. A woman with red lipstick, who didn't know he'd recently returned from overseas or that his name appeared on a list of soldiers killed in action.

Jonas leaned back in his seat and picked up the newspaper that someone had left behind, along with a magazine. He'd already read both cover to cover but it gave him something to hide behind. Privacy to plan his *next step without answering questions that travelers so often asked out of basic curiosity. He could keep it between himself and the driver that he had a ticket to St. Louis.*

Only he knew that he wasn't reading an article about why Americans would need to continue rationing sugar, but making a mental list of what he would need once he reached his destination.

A place to stay.

A job.

A new name.

He couldn't get a job or even be trusted to rent a room without a name.

Jonas flipped the page to a section with wedding announcements and obituaries. He closed his eyes. The first man's name I point to will be my first name, at least for now. He pointed to the page and opened his eyes.

Abraham.

Abraham made him sound like an old man with gray hairs growing out of his ears.

He closed his eyes to try again. Until he realized that an old man's name would be the perfect cover. He read Abraham's obituary. Abraham Gleeson had died at age ninety-five of natural causes, leaving behind his wife of seventy-five years, Mable, three sons, eight grandchildren, twelve great-grandchildren, and four great-great-grandchildren. He would be remembered as a loving father, husband, grandfather, and friend, who spent his retirement years driving a school bus, contributing to the war effort as an air raid warden, and teaching Sunday school.

Abe Gleeson sounded like a great man.

Abe. I don't mind being an Abe. After all, Abraham was one of the patriarchs of the Bible. A man of great faith. I sure need that.

Now for a last name.

His finger landed on Winker.

He had to work so hard not to laugh that he let out a snort, and a little boy across the aisle laughed. I have control over very little right now. I am not settling for a last name like Winker.

He took another stab at the obituary section. He opened his eyes to the name Halner.

Mildred Halner passed away peacefully surrounded by her family after a brief illness...

He searched his jacket pocket and found a pencil that he'd sharpened down to the stub during his senior year of high school. In the other pocket, behind Gracie's postcard, he found a folded sheet of notebook paper. He unfolded it. A vocabulary quiz from French class. He'd gotten a seventy-eight percent. Communicating with the DeSmetts in their native tongue might have been easier from the get-go if he'd applied himself more in French class.

He turned the paper over and wrote Abraham Halner.

I need a middle name.

He so wanted to choose his father's name. But it felt too dangerous. So he chose something generic. John.

Abraham John Halner.

Abraham J Halner

Abe Halner.

He practiced his new name in printing and cursive, with the middle name or initial and without, until the bus pulled into another rest stop. He put the old quiz paper back into his pocket. He walked to a hamburger stand at the rest stop and checked his supply of cash. His stomach cried out for a burger, french fries, and an ice-cold soda. But his need to make his money stretch forced him to opt for the burger and a cup to fill with water at the drinking fountain. At the fountain, he removed the French quiz and the postcard from his pocket.

He mouthed, "I love you, Gracie" before tearing the Brooklyn Bridge right down the middle and then in fourths.

He tore up the quiz as well. He ripped Jonas Townsend, Period 5 *off and into tiny pieces before crumbling the quiz sheet and his last note to Gracie into his fist and dropped the ball into the trash can on the way to the bus.*

The bus driver honked the horn. "Five minutes. Next stop, St. Louis."

Jonas boarded the bus with his burger bag in one hand and tried not to slosh his cup of water. He nodded to the bus driver on his way up the steps.

"We'll be in St. Louis in one hour, tops."

"Thanks a lot. It'll be good to be home."

Jonas rehearsed a dialogue in his mind.

"Do you have a room for the night?"

"We have one as long as you don't mind a crying baby upstairs. Can I have your name?"

"Abe Halner."

The army would likely never know that by prematurely declaring him dead, they might have saved his life.

CHAPTER TWENTY

*J*anet's eyes were starting to cross after two hours of reading letter after letter and talking through what each page added to the story of a young man returning from war only to leave his life in Dennison behind for another that he built from scratch. All out of his desire to protect his father's legacy and the woman he loved. With only the DeSmetts' side of the mail exchange and brief notes from Abe's notebook to work with, they'd had to fill in many blanks with speculation.

Laney removed her reading glasses and rubbed her eyes.

"How you doing?" Janet asked. All three of them had gotten a bit tearful when they realized why Abe Halner had Jonas Townsend's identification and possessions in a safe-deposit box.

"I'm okay." Laney's eyes were misty and tired but also peaceful. "It's a relief to know my grandfather didn't have his identity stolen as Mom feared. And he didn't do something illegal that would shatter my wonderful memories of him. But I wish we could learn what he went through before meeting Grandma Ivy. I adored him already, and knowing his whole story would have made me love him even more. Instead, he carried this secret around for nearly eighty years— most of his life." She reached for the box of letters from the DeSmetts. "At least he didn't carry the burden completely alone. I'm glad he told Edda. And based on the postmark, he told her shortly after arriving in St. Louis."

Janet took the letter out to read it again. "Edda DeSmett was an amazing woman. I don't know if I would have been brave enough to keep a wounded soldier hidden in my home after already losing my husband in a war, having my son return wounded from fighting those who'd taken over my country, and struggling to feed my children. Then to get a letter from that soldier, saying he had to flee his hometown and change his name because of a threatening letter connected to a debt his dad accrued? I would probably say, 'I am so sorry,' and focus on my own family's needs. Which I'm sure were numerous for Edda after the Nazi occupation ended."

But Edda had not done that.

Oh, Jonas, my heart is breaking for you. You have my promise that I will keep your confidence and do my best to explain to the children why they are to now address their notes and pictures to Abe. To us, you will always be our dear friend Jonas, and as I said when you left our home, our door is always open to you...

Debbie handed a letter across the table. "Laney, look at this one. The DeSmetts might not have been the only ones who kept Jonas's secret. This one is from 1947."

Laney rolled her shoulders and reached one hand up and around the back of her neck to give herself a massage. Her hand stopped as she read. "I think you're right. It sounds like Grandma Ivy knew. If Grandpa listened to Edda here."

"What did she say?" Janet asked.

"'Your new girlfriend, Ivy, sounds wonderful. I am so grateful that you have found love again after so much loss. But may I give you a word of advice? Please forgive me if I am crossing the lines of friendship. I feel that you must tell Ivy the truth about your identity. Since the end of the war, many people have tried to hide parts of their lives. Choices they made that they're not proud of. Experiences that changed them forever. I have seen good friends, and even love, torn apart by secrets that came to light. I have learned that relationships cannot be based on lies. You changed your name not because you wanted to hide something you did wrong, but because someone else did wrong, and you wanted to protect those you hold dear.'"

"There's a lot of wisdom in that," Debbie said.

"Edda continues, 'If Ivy truly loves you, the truth will not change that love. She might be upset at first, but she will come around, and if you ask her to, she will protect your secret as I have.'" Laney smiled and handed the letter to Janet. "Now I know why Grandma called Grandpa's occasional road trips 'alone time.' She was keeping his confidence. My grandparents had been married for over sixty years when Grandma passed away. As far as I know, she went to her grave without telling a soul that her husband's given name was Jonas."

Janet ran a fingertip over Edda DeSmett's faded cursive, her wisdom so gentle and courageous. She had blessed Jonas's life for so many years.

Laney returned the letter to the shoebox.

Janet pulled a letter out of the box that Laney had found under Abe's bed. They'd only gotten to a few of them so far. "Is it okay if I read this one?"

"Of course." Laney put the lid on the letters she'd found in the safe-deposit box.

> *Dear Abe,*
>
> *It was such a blessing to see you during your anniversary holiday and finally meet your wife, Ivy. I only wish the children could have been here.*

"Laney, this is so cool. Your grandmother met Edda." Janet read the entire letter aloud to Laney and Debbie. At the time of the visit, Mila was studying art in Rome and planning a wedding for the following June, and Oskar had started university.

"Oh, wow. You have no idea how helpful that letter will be." Laney squeezed her eyes shut and laughed. "It officially clears up a question my mom had. While going through Grandpa's things a few weeks ago, Mom found a framed picture of him with a woman. Grandpa had passed, and Grandma had been gone for years, so Mom couldn't ask either of them who the woman was. Of course, because she was grieving, the picture rattled her. She called me in tears, thinking her dad might have had an affair. She told me she'd opened the frame and found a note on the back that said, 'With Edda, Bastogne, Belgium, European trip, September 1960.'"

"That's so special," Debbie said with a smile. "Though I understand the assumption."

"I reminded Mom that Grandma was in Belgium with Grandpa in 1960, during their tenth-anniversary trip to Europe. They constantly told stories about that trip. I told Mom that Edda might have been someone they met during their travels and that Grandma probably took the photo. That calmed her down. We agreed that if Grandpa had an inappropriate relationship with a woman named Edda, he most likely would not have kept the picture on a shelf in the living room where anyone could find it. She felt silly. I told her I probably would have reacted the same way if I found a picture of Dad with a woman who wasn't her. She made me promise not to repeat that story at her funeral, and we both had a good laugh."

"It truly is the best medicine," Janet said.

Laney leaned back and yawned. "I need to tell Mom she can stop wondering about that picture on Grandpa's photo album shelf now. I can also fill her in on who Edda was."

Janet put Edda's letter on the table in front of her. "How about if we call it a day and tackle the rest tomorrow after my last session with the future baking stars of America?"

Laney stretched her arms over her head. "That would be great. I could use a break to process all this. I also want to call my mom and fill her in on what we've discovered."

Debbie put away the papers. "Greg was hoping I would drop by his house tonight so Julian can try out his contest entry on me. That's not cheating, right?"

Janet found a shopping bag for Laney to take the two shoeboxes of letters home in, along with everything else from the safe-deposit box. There was too much to fit in her tote bag now. "Not at all. I think it's great that Julian thought of practicing ahead of time to perfect what he wants to make. He just can't practice on Harry, Ray, Eileen, or me."

"Thank goodness." Debbie snapped the last lid in place.

Janet helped Laney stack her grandfather's things in the bag. "Let me know if you want company or help reading the other letters from the DeSmetts."

"I will. You know what I'm the most curious about now, though?"

Janet set the bag on the floor beside Laney's purse. "What's that?"

"I want to know more about that C.B. person, the one who left that threatening note for Jonas. Or I guess I should say my grandpa." Laney folded her reading glasses and held them against her chest. "It feels so strange to say that. To know that my grandpa Abe went by another name for the first twenty years of his life." She picked up her purse and slid her glasses into a pink quilted pouch. "But you know what? That is exactly why I want more information. I want to get to the bottom of what happened. If it's even possible after so many years."

After cleaning up the kitchen and dining room, with Ian working late at the police station, Janet forced herself to focus on creating a fun last presentation for the Culinary Arts Club. It was tougher than she expected, since all she wanted to do was comb the internet for information that she might be able to pass on to Laney about the car accident that had killed Jonas's parents.

When she saw a request from Miranda Sloan for a video call to go over the contest details, she knew her search would have to wait. At eight o'clock, Janet hit the meeting link, hoping Miranda wouldn't mind that she was reclining against her headboard. When the teacher's video came on, Janet discovered that she had also chosen the head of her bed for the call, her hair pulled back and no makeup on.

"The kids and I are so excited about this." Miranda adjusted her screen, revealing Sycamore State Park sweatshirt. "It's unique and fun, and the parents love the idea of some of the oldest members of the community judging the entries."

"I am so glad the parents like the idea, because our judges can hardly wait. They feel so important right now."

"Well, they should." Miranda put on a pair of big, purple-framed glasses. "Let me make sure we're on the same page as far as the rules. It'll be a blind tasting, meaning the judges won't know who baked each entry until they announce the winner. I emailed the students a permission slip and my standard contract for projects. Would you like to add anything else?"

"I know of at least one student who is taking time to practice on his dad. I want to make sure it is okay to encourage the kids to do that."

"I don't see why not. I like that they want to practice and make their recipe better."

"Excellent. And Earth's Market donated two gift cards, so we can have a winner and a runner-up."

"Are you serious? That means so much to me. Janet, your contribution to the club is surpassing my expectations."

"It's surpassing mine too." *To think we got to this contest from mini muffins that fell flat.* "I'm having a blast."

Janet wrapped up the call and shut her laptop then got up to let Laddie out for the last time before going to bed. Ranger sat beside his food dish, yowling as if he hadn't eaten in days.

"Oh, you poor thing." Janet let Laddie back in and picked up Ranger's dish. She was filling it when her phone rang. She hurried to set the dish down and grabbed her phone off the counter. Laney's name appeared on the screen. "Hey, Laney. What's up?"

Laney jumped right in. "Janet, I think the car accident that killed Jonas's parents was intentional. I went to the library and looked it up in their newspaper archives."

Janet pulled out a kitchen chair and sat down. "What did you find?"

Laney took a deep breath. "One article detailed the accident, but it also included information about Larry and Bridget Townsend—how long the family had resided in Dennison, that sort of thing. Janet, Larry Townsend was a trained auto mechanic. Yet, his brakes failed on the interstate?"

"I know. Ray told me the situation always seemed strange to him. He said Jonas's dad was meticulous about his car."

"Why didn't anyone investigate the accident further? A trained mechanic who was known for being meticulous about his car wouldn't neglect his brakes."

"Why indeed?" Janet murmured.

Even though it would mean less sleep before her early alarm clock, Janet waited up for Ian to come home so she could tell him about Laney's call over a cup of bedtime tea. "Laney has a point. A mechanic's brakes failing doesn't add up."

Ian squeezed out his tea bag and set it on a plate. "You must remember that Larry and Bridget's accident happened in 1943. Investigators didn't have all the technology and knowledge they have now. Cars didn't include computer systems that reminded the driver to schedule a routine service or alerted them about an issue. Even today, if the brakes failed on a car and caused a fatal accident, I wouldn't suspect foul play unless I had a legitimate reason to."

"Even if the driver was a trained mechanic?"

Ian gave a little shrug and took a sip of his tea. "I'm no expert on cars, but my guess is that a person can keep up with routine maintenance and still have something go wrong. We don't always know what is about to fail."

"But it's possible that someone could have tampered with it."

"Sure, it's possible. And trust me, after what you've told me about Jonas's letters, I'm just as suspicious as you are. But if the police didn't suspect foul play when the accident happened, it will be hard to connect the incident to a specific criminal over eighty years later."

Ian's point kept Janet awake half the night. Even if someone could prove foul play, what justice could be served? The perpetrator likely wasn't alive anymore, nor were his victims.

In the morning at the café, Janet baked cinnamon buns and took them out to the counter. The morning after very little sleep called for something scrumptious to bake.

Debbie set a breakfast order on the counter. "One ham and egg scramble with cheddar cheese and extra-crispy home fries."

"Coming right up as soon as I get these into the case." She put the order in her apron pocket and squatted down to slide the morning buns into the bottom rack.

"What do you think you're doing?"

Janet almost whacked her head on the top of the bakery case. "Excuse me?"

The man's voice was familiar but not so much that she could immediately put a face to the angry tone or figure out why he felt the need to bark at her in front of other customers.

Janet shut the case and stood up to find Rodd Nickles at the counter, wearing a fierce scowl.

She tried to defuse the tension. "Do you mean what am I doing right this minute? I think I'm adding more buns to the bakery case."

"You know that isn't what I mean."

Janet set aside the empty tray and wiped her hands on her apron. "To be honest, Rodd, I don't know what you mean. But I would be happy to listen. You seem upset."

"I *am* upset. I just dropped my granddaughter off at school and listened to her go on and on about how cool it was that you asked her to translate an old letter the other day. A letter written to Jonas Townsend, who happens to be connected to the house that the preservation society is interested in purchasing. She was also excited about the possibility of helping you more if other letters in the big box you have turn out to include some French as well."

Janet glanced at Debbie, who raised her eyebrows in a silent question. *Do you need me to come over there and rescue you with an urgent request for assistance?*

She gave her friend a subtle headshake and took the breakfast order out of her pocket. "If you can wait about ten minutes so I can make this scramble, I will meet you out in the depot where we can talk privately." Paulette was due to arrive any minute, so it wouldn't be a big deal if she took a break.

Rodd turned on his heel without a word, passing Paulette on his way out the door. Janet gave her as much time to check in and get settled as she would on any other day. She was not going to make someone else's mood a café emergency.

She finished the scramble, allowing the sizzle of eggs and diced ham to calm her spirit, handed the kitchen over to Debbie and Paulette, and then braced herself to find out why Rodd had been so reactive this morning. She found him sitting on a bench, staring at the image of Bing the War Dog on the museum ticket counter.

Janet sat beside him. "Rodd, I am sorry if I overstepped. I was under the impression that Bethany's mom gave her permission to help me with that letter."

Harry walked into the depot with Crosby and waved to Janet on his way into the café. She waved back, prompting Rodd to glance over his shoulder and give Harry a friendly wave as well.

Once the café door closed, Rodd faced Janet and spoke quietly, but his voice held the same intensity as before. "Yes, I know. I asked Bethany if her parents knew about the letter, and she told me they were fine with it. But I can tell you right now, if they'd known the details of the project, I doubt they would have allowed her to help you. Anything could have been in that letter. Bethany is thirteen years old."

"Rodd, I raised a daughter. I wouldn't have asked an eighth grader for help without an idea of what she might find, and I would have stopped her immediately if the letter had gone in an inappropriate direction. But I understand your frustration."

The anger on Rodd's face melted away, replaced by an expression that Janet couldn't quite put her finger on. "Why translate the French at all? From what I understand, it came from a stack of old mail that you and Laney found in a safe-deposit box. It's not as if Laney needs proof of her grandfather's connection to the house. It won't change anything when it comes to the sale."

"This is not about the house," Janet said calmly. "It's about Laney uncovering the truth about her grandfather. Why the grandfather she loved seemed to be keeping secrets. If a member of your family turned out to be someone originally listed as killed in action but seemed to live on for decades after that, wouldn't you want to know what happened?"

"Yes. I suppose I would."

"And if the man listed as killed in action also happened to have lost both of his parents in a suspicious car accident, wouldn't you be a bit curious about that as well?"

Rodd suddenly seemed to lose the ability to form a response. "Why dig up that part? Again, it has nothing to do with the house or who will ultimately buy it."

"Because if her grandfather and Jonas Townsend are the same person, Laney would like to know what happened to her grandfather's parents."

"She knows what happened to Jonas's parents. It's in the public records. They died in a car accident in 1943."

"Based on what many who knew Jonas remember, the circumstances are suspect."

"You know it's very possible that the accident wasn't suspicious at all. Car accidents happen all the time. That was as true in 1943 as it is now."

Janet watched another regular enter the café and longed to go back in to make pancakes and catch up with locals. She didn't think this conversation was going to be very productive. "This is a big deal to Laney."

"Yes, I get that. But sometimes the truth is best left alone."

Janet watched Rodd's face for any indication of why someone's desire for answers put him so on edge. "I'm afraid I disagree with you there. It all depends on why someone wants to avoid the truth and why it got covered up at all. The truth will always come out."

Was it her imagination, or had some of the color drained from his face at her words?

CHAPTER TWENTY-ONE

*A*round midmorning, Laney came into the café. The dark circles under her eyes told Janet she'd gotten as little sleep as Janet had and desperately needed a cup of coffee.

"Hi, Laney," Janet said. "How are you doing this morning?"

"Okay. I'm still trying to make sense of all we discovered during our letter-reading extravaganza and the information I found at the library." She settled onto a stool and unzipped her navy sweatshirt. "It's a lot."

"I've been feeling for you ever since we hung up last night." As she'd told Ian after their discussion about the accident, it was one thing for Laney to find out that her grandfather had secrets and another to discover that he was living under an assumed name. Then to read the old article about the accident. "What can I get for you?"

"Just some coffee for now."

Debbie came over and gave Laney a hug. "Good morning. Did you get a chance to talk to your mom?"

"I called her last night and told her everything. Then she wanted to talk again this morning. She told me that once the whole story sank in, she could look back and see the signs all over the place. Her father's road trips that Grandma supported but never explained. He never took advantage of veteran benefits. And he didn't have any pictures of himself from childhood, or of his parents. Mom said she always thought her father lost everything in a house fire. He didn't tell her that, but she created the story in her mind."

Debbie handed Laney her coffee and leaned against the counter as she listened.

Laney added vanilla creamer to her coffee. "I went through Grandpa Abe's notebook again before walking over here and noticed a photo that I think might be another piece of the puzzle. It's a picture of a park bench with some kind of plaque on it that I couldn't read. When I turned the picture over, I saw the address of a park in Barnhill. I'm going to meet Mom there tomorrow, so we can check it out."

"Maybe that will give you some more answers," Janet said.

"I hope so." Laney stirred her coffee and took a long sip. "I'm thankful that Jonas created a happy life for himself as Abe Halner. But the reason he had to breaks my heart." She stared down into her cup. "I told Brian about the article I found. He told me failed brakes could happen to anyone."

Janet waved as a group of women left the café, leaving it empty. "Ian told me the same thing. It doesn't mean they weren't tampered with, only that it's impossible to prove at this point."

"I'm trying to focus on being thankful that Jonas Townsend didn't die in the war. I wouldn't be sitting here right now if he hadn't moved to St. Louis and met my grandmother at a potluck."

The bell on the front door jingled. Debbie gave Laney a gentle pat on the back as she went to greet the two elderly women who came in.

"I don't want to keep you," Laney said to Janet. "I'm going to finish my coffee, and then I can call you later if I learn anything new."

"Stay as long as you want." Janet added some hot coffee to Laney's mug as a sign that she meant what she said.

Debbie came back to the counter for the coffeepot. "Hey, Janet, I thought of someone who would like to know that Jonas Townsend survived the war."

A beloved veteran's face popped into her mind. "Ray."

Laney took another creamer from the basket. "That's right. I would love to be with you when you tell him."

Janet mentally went over her schedule for the afternoon. "I'll have some free time between when I leave here and when I'm due at the Culinary Arts Club meeting. How about if we go to Good Shepherd together to give Ray the news?"

"Sounds good," Laney agreed. "In the meantime, I'm going to check public records to confirm whether Grandpa legally changed his name or lived under an alias. My mom could really use the information for all the paperwork she and her siblings are dealing with right now."

Janet prepared to return to the griddle. "All righty then. This afternoon, you and me." She saw a hint of weariness in Laney's eyes and reached across the counter to pat her shoulder. "And don't let what we heard about faulty brakes get you down too much. If there is more to that accident than what the original report says, we will find out somehow."

As soon as Janet turned onto the road to Good Shepherd, Laney rolled the window down. "This place is beautiful." She leaned her head partway out the window while Janet found a parking space. "My mom is in her early seventies, and I'd say she's still a decade or so away from needing assisted living. But when she does, I hope she finds a place like this."

Janet shut off her car. "Wait until you see the inside. It's so homey, and everyone who works here is lovely."

"I forgot to tell you on the way here. I looked into Grandpa's name change, and he legally changed it in 1947, which was the year he met my grandmother."

"That lines up with the letter we saw from Edda, encouraging your grandpa to be honest with Ivy."

Laney picked up her purse and got out of the car. "I always admired my grandma, but I never appreciated how incredible she was until now. A lot of women in her situation would have gotten scared with the story of the threatening note and broken things off."

"That's how I might have reacted." Janet opened the entrance to Good Shepherd and held it for Laney.

Ray was already waiting in the visiting area nearest the door. "Good afternoon, ladies."

Janet leaned down to give Ray a hug. "Hi, Ray."

Laney held her hand out to him. "It's so nice to see you again."

"It's nice to see you too. Janet tells me you have some news to share. I'm eager to hear it. How about if we go into the dayroom?"

Janet took hold of the handles on the back of Ray's wheelchair. "That sounds good to me."

Ray settled in as they made their way down the hall toward the room where residents enjoyed hanging out or attending the many activities the center arranged for them. "One of the volunteers was in there adding fall decorations, and I heard a rumor about her putting out some snacks and coffee."

"I can't wait to see it," Janet said. "What's Eileen up to today?"

"She's visiting with a new resident. Apparently they went to high school together."

Janet smiled. Maybe some girl talk would alert Eileen to a certain sweet man's crush. "I bet they'll have a lot to catch up on."

Laney explored the dayroom while Janet pushed Ray to a round table in a corner by the window with a nice view of evergreen trees and one of the walking paths.

"So, what brings you ladies over on a sunny afternoon when you could be out galivanting?" Ray asked.

Laney chose the chair beside Ray's wheelchair. "Well, you know I've been researching why my grandfather had a photograph of the Townsend house in his notebook."

"Yes. Did you figure it out?"

"I did, and—well, I'm not sure where to start, so maybe I should simply say it." She folded her hands on the table. "My grandfather, Abe Halner, had a picture of Jonas's house because he was Jonas Townsend. He survived the war."

Ray stared at her. "What? But he was listed as killed."

"That was a mistake. We figured all this out through brief notes he wrote and letters he received from a woman named Edda DeSmett, so it's a bit confusing. We're still sorting through it all. What we do know is that Jonas was wounded in the Bastogne region of Belgium in late December 1944, which would have placed him at the Battle of the Bulge as reported. But then he spent time with Edda and her family in that area. Grandpa mentions a man named Chip in his notebook, and something about covering Chip with his over-coat. So I'm assuming Chip was mistaken for Jonas."

Janet watched Ray's face as Laney told him about the threatening letter they found, and the bits of information they'd pieced together around her dining room table.

When Laney finished, Ray gazed out the window for a while, clearly digesting what she'd said. Finally, he let out a long, soft whistle. "My friend survived. So that morning, when I thought I saw Jonas leaving his parents' house, I wasn't imagining things."

"No you weren't," Janet said. "Neither was Harry when he thought he saw Jonas at the train station."

Ray kept his gaze on the window. "I wish Jonas had told me he was in trouble. I would have taken him to the police station to report the letter. Instead, he went through that frightening situation all alone."

"He was afraid for Gracie," Laney told him. "So he went to St. Louis. That's where he met my grandmother, Ivy Carson. They married in 1950 and relocated to Cincinnati. He had three kids, and eight grandkids, including me. He had a long life and a loving family."

Ray chin trembled as if he was fighting tears. "He always wanted kids."

Janet found a box of tissues near the television and set it in front of Ray. "Are you okay?"

"Yeah, I'm all right. This is quite a shock. It's a relief to know Jonas survived the war, though I'm sad I missed the rest of his life. The reason he left Dennison is hard to think about. Jonas once confided in me that he thought his father might have gotten involved in something shady."

"Did he mention what it was?"

"He heard his father say something about a card game. But he also said his dad wasn't a big gambler, so he didn't know for sure. Did anyone ever find out who sent that threatening letter? Based on what Jonas told me and what you've learned, I think whoever wrote it was responsible for Larry and Bridget's accident."

Janet wanted so badly to be able to give him a different answer. "Not as far as we know. It was so long ago."

Laney leaned across the table and squeezed Ray's arm. "But I plan to figure it out if at all possible. We both deserve peace, which comes with answers."

Janet pushed Ray's wheelchair along the walking path behind Good Shepherd.

"Getting out for a walk was a good idea. Thanks for suggesting it." Ray took a deep breath and gestured toward the evergreens that surrounded the main building. "Fall is a wonderful time of year for being outdoors. The air gets that damp, earthy smell to it. Soon the leaves will start changing and falling like colorful blessings. I remember my first fall after coming home from the war. School had started for the kids, but for me, life felt so untethered."

"I can't imagine how hard it must have been for you and all those other men to adjust to normal life after a war. You were all so young."

The word *young* struck Janet right in the heart. Ray had been younger than Tiffany when he'd left Dennison to fight in a foreign country, not knowing if he would return.

"Yeah, we were a bunch of kids who'd been thrown into a grown-up situation. I don't think any of us truly understood what we were up against until we faced it. When the war ended, we came home expecting life to return to normal. It was hard for all of us."

Janet couldn't imagine.

"When I was fighting, all I wanted to do was get home. Somehow, I thought it would be the same as I left it," Ray went on. "But once I stepped off the train at Dennison Station, everything had changed. I'd been injured while fighting in the British Isles and had a long recovery from that. I knew I was fortunate that my injury hadn't killed me. I knew far too many men—many of them still teenagers—who weren't coming home."

"Friends like Jonas." The words came out of Janet's mouth as little more than a whisper.

"That's right. I found out about his alleged passing when I was in a military hospital in England getting ready to head home. I'd already heard about his parents in a letter from my mother."

Laney put her hands into her sweatshirt pockets. "I read that Jonas's dad was a mechanic. Is that right?"

"He was trained as one, and at one time he tried to open his own auto repair shop here in town, but it never got off the ground."

"Did it strike you as strange that he knew so much about cars but died because his brakes failed?" Laney asked.

Ray blinked in surprise. "At the time, I didn't even think about that. But you're right. It is strange. I can't believe I never thought of it before."

"You had a lot to think about back then," Laney said sympathetically.

"Yes, I did. Losing Jonas after what happened to his parents didn't seem real. Until I came home and saw their empty house. The tree that we climbed as boys. The driveway where Jonas's mom let us sell lemonade to earn some spending money over the summer when we were ten. Hearing that Gracie Pike was engaged to another man. Everything and everyone seemed to have left Jonas and his family in the past. It broke my heart."

"Understandably," Janet said.

Ray patted the arms of his chair. "One day in mid-October, I went for a walk, feeling sorry for myself. And all of a sudden, leaves from a maple tree fell all around me like rain. I stopped and let them fall. I felt sure that it was God saying, 'I have plans for you, Ray. Don't you worry. You've been through some hard things, but I can redeem all that.'"

Janet spotted a maple tree that would soon start to change and drop its leaves, and imagined Ray as a young man, barely out of childhood and yet having been through a lifetime of hardship, standing under it.

Laney laid a hand on Ray's shoulder. "Maybe my grandpa had a moment like that too."

"I bet he did. God is good that way."

Janet felt a sense of relief that Jonas didn't have to see his girl with someone else. "Where did Gracie end up?"

"When I came home from Europe, the Pikes had left Dennison. Gracie had gone to stay with her sister after she got the news of Jonas's death. Then her brother was badly wounded, and her parents went to be close to him in Dayton. They all returned in the summer of 1945—after Jonas was home and left again. Gracie eventually married a man from Uhrichsville. It didn't surprise anyone to see her find love again, and we were all happy for her. Gracie was sweet and pretty and full of life. She caught the eye of one of her brother's friends, Glen Murray. He was a good man. Jonas would've been happy to know they ended up together."

"Glen Murray? Any relation to Christine Murray?"

"That's right," Ray told Janet. "Glen and Gracie's oldest son, Clayton, is Christine's dad."

Janet saw a bench under a shade tree and pushed Ray's chair over to it so they could talk in a way that gave his neck a break. "Well, that is an interesting bit of trivia."

Laney sat on the bench across from Ray. "When did Jonas's house go up for sale?"

"Soon after the war ended."

"Did you know the family that turned it into a boardinghouse?"

"Not well initially. It was Chad Grayson's great-uncle, who was new to Dennison at the time. He and his sister and her little boy came from the East Coast after the war. They did a nice job with it. Laney, you asked me how I got retethered. The boardinghouse had a big part in that process. I started going over there to visit with the men, and before I knew it, I was volunteering to play piano for them on Saturday nights. It started with one of the fellas inviting me to play at a party and became a regular thing."

Janet sat beside Laney. "I don't think I've ever heard this story."

"I guess I never had a reason to tell it. But with all the talk about Jonas's house, it has come to mind a lot lately."

Janet checked the time, wishing it would stand still so she and Laney could sit in the sunshine talking to Ray for as long as they wanted to. For now, they had forty-five minutes left before she had to head over to the middle school again, and she planned to enjoy every second of it.

Laney settled back on the bench. "I bet it felt good to do something like that after so much fighting, loss, and uncertainty."

"I don't think I fully appreciated the difference it made at the time. I knew it made me feel good, plus helped me get my mind off all the bad memories I had from the war. Playing music made me smile and laugh when I once thought I'd never do either again. Life felt good and joyful again."

"That must have made a world of difference for you," Janet said.

"It did. One Saturday night when I was playing, a guy I knew from high school—who struggled with what we now know as PTSD—asked if I minded him joining me on guitar. He'd been teaching himself to play. I said, 'Sure. Why not?' Next thing I knew, other guys started showing up with old instruments that had been collecting dust, and we had ourselves a band."

Janet marveled over how a visit to share one piece of information could grow into a deep conversation that allowed her to get to know her friend better. "I had no idea you were a music star back in the day."

He ducked his head, blushing. "Well, we weren't quite that cool. But we did have some fun times. We had a saxophone and a trombone, and even a kid with an old set of bongos." The face that had looked so sad when they left the dayroom started contorting in uncontrollable laughter. "Once we got so loud that the old ladies down the street called the cops on us for disturbing the peace. My folks got word of it, and you would have thought I was twelve years old again."

"You never stop being a parent," Laney said with a chuckle.

"Even at the time, I knew Mom was embarrassed more than anything else. 'I hope you weren't drinking with those band members of yours,' she said. I teased her, 'We were, Mom. We were drinking cola floats. One guy brought over some pretzels.' Then Dad piped in, 'Sounds like a wild scene. Wish I could've been there.' Dad and I cracked up, and Mom did too. Then she said, 'It sure feels good to laugh, doesn't it?' And that was the end of that." Ray grinned. "Until Mom saw the woman who called the cops in the grocery store and scolded her for making such a fuss over a little music after we guys fought so hard for others' freedom overseas."

"It's too bad we can't fit a piano in the café," Janet said. "We'd have you come over and entertain the customers."

"I've gotten kind of rusty," Ray said. "But I like to noodle around on the upright piano in the dayroom sometimes. Now I'm tempted to see how many of those guys from the boardinghouse band are still around. We could get our band going again. My neck is feeling better if we want to keep going."

As Janet pushed his wheelchair along the path, she noticed Ray growing quiet again. "How are you doing? Getting tired?"

"Nah, I'm just thinking."

"About what?" Laney asked.

"I was wondering about Jonas. I know he wasn't the only soldier mistakenly reported as KIA. It happened sometimes before they had all the testing and technology that they use now. I've read such stories before you told me about Jonas. All we really had for ID were our dog tags, and they certainly weren't indestructible. But what about the other soldier? The man Jonas covered with his coat? Was he reported as MIA? Or did his family become one of those who never found out what happened to their loved one?"

Laney watched the sky for a moment. "That's a good question. Other than the sentence about covering Chip with his coat, Grandpa Abe never mentioned him again."

Janet slowed her pace while considering Ray's question. "I hope his family got answers. But I don't know how they could have, nor do I have the faintest idea where we would start trying to track them down."

In Janet's car, Laney buckled her seat belt. "I like Ray. He's such a delight to be around."

Janet tossed her purse into the back seat. "I saw a whole new side of him today." She struggled to control her laughter while preparing to pull out of the parking space. "I cannot wait to tell Debbie he was in a band. I'm going home right now to order him a coffee mug with a music theme."

"It should say 'Rock on.'"

"Yes! With some of those flying piano keyboards and an electric guitar. He'll use it proudly, I'm sure."

She pulled out of the Good Shepherd parking lot and considered all that she, Laney, and Ray had covered in their visit. "Do you find it interesting that Christine Murray is related to the man who married Jonas's girlfriend, Gracie?"

"I absolutely do. Especially considering how determined Christine is to outbid Brian and me. Or rather, to raise questions about our character, so we aren't trusted enough to bid at all."

"You knew about that?"

"Don't worry. Christine didn't contact me or anything. I heard about it through Rodd. He thought it would be a good idea for us to know in case Christine did reach out directly. He also wanted us to be prepared for a bidding war once the house officially goes up for sale."

"Maybe it's better that you found out, so you didn't get blind-sided." Janet headed toward the depot to drop Laney off at the Pullman. "I wish I could understand what Christine is so upset about. There are other old houses up for sale in Dennison, including a Georgian-style home that's in better shape than the Townsend house. We now know that Jonas Townsend was your grandfather, so she can't accuse you of making up stories. But why do it in the first place? Legally you still don't have any more right to the house than the Dennison Preservation Society does."

"Even if my grandfather's connection to the house could give me first dibs on a bid, I wouldn't expect to get the house based on that. I would want to buy it fair and square. Otherwise I'd always wonder if I really deserved it," Laney said. "I know it's wrong to judge other people's motives, especially considering Christine's assumptions about me. But maybe *she* feels a sense of ownership of the house. Think about it. If my grandfather hadn't found that threatening letter, he would have told the army that he had not been killed in Belgium. He would have married Gracie Pike, and the house would be part of Christine's family legacy. Instead, it went up for auction. Now is her chance to have the house."

"If that were the case, Christine would have to know about her grandma's relationship with Jonas. My grandparents never talked about people they dated before meeting their spouses—did yours?" Janet asked.

Laney relaxed against the headrest. "That's true. If I hadn't emptied that safe-deposit box, I wouldn't know my grandfather once loved Gracie."

Janet considered Laney's scenario, and the many ramifications of what could have happened if Jonas hadn't found that letter demanding payment of his father's debt. "If Gracie had married Jonas Townsend, Christine wouldn't exist. So she should be thankful that things turned out the way they did."

"That is such a weird thought. But you're right." Laney covered her face with a groan. "In that scenario, I wouldn't exist either. I wouldn't be here talking to you right now. Now my brain hurts."

"Oh. Yeah. Sorry about that."

"So if genetics can't explain Christine's reaction to my wanting the house, what does?"

"Christine has always been very passionate about her community involvement. She never married, which means she also doesn't have kids." Janet thought more deeply about that. "She's in her mid-forties like me, so some of her friends are starting to talk about grandkids, and she won't experience that. I've heard her say the Dennison Preservation Society is her baby."

"And a newcomer arriving out of the blue to buy the house for a themed B and B disrupted her plan for the Dennison House."

"Yes, but to be fair, the preservation society's plan for the Dennison House didn't include a contract of any kind. If I understood Greg Connor correctly, the Graysons are waiting for some inspections before putting the house up for sale. They promised to seriously consider the preservation society's offer when the time comes, nothing more. But yes, she probably did see you as a threat."

"I know Brian and I probably came across as con artists, showing up at the café with a photo, a notebook filled with random stories, and our dream of opening a themed B and B."

"Well, as we talked about the other day, this is a small town. Word had already gone around about the preservation society's plan, so people decided that was what was happening. And then there you were, presenting a totally different possibility. I think it just caught people off guard," Janet said.

"Our out-there themed B and B probably pales in comparison to Christine's idea for a museum. If I were the Graysons, I know who I would choose to sell to."

"Your idea isn't that out there. The Pullmans are a themed B and B, and nobody calls them tacky." Then Janet caught herself. "I mean—"

"It's okay. I've already heard the rumor that Christine thinks my idea is tacky."

"Well, Debbie and I think your B and B sounds cute. Maybe the community could have it and the Dennison House Museum. It has a historic feel and would probably draw tourists, which is always a hit around here." Janet passed the depot. "Whatever Christine's motives are for getting in your way, I want to help you find all the answers you need about your grandfather. Including who was threatening him and whether there is a connection between the letter and what happened to his parents." She parked in front of the Pullman.

"I appreciate that a lot." Laney grabbed her tote bag. "My heart tells me there is a connection. That line about how unfortunate it would be for Jonas to suffer the same fate as his parents is a giveaway."

Janet thought about Patricia's story about the case study she heard during law school. "And criminals do have ways of disguising murders as accidents."

Laney reached for the door handle then stopped. "If we find out who is responsible for my grandfather's parents' death, that could provide answers about other suspicious deaths in the area. Other families could have their questions answered once and for all."

"That would be wonderful, wouldn't it? Jonas's KIA status left one other family with questions they may never have answered, but this could be bigger than that. Who knows how many families were affected by this? If Jonas's parents' accident did involve foul play, it's too late for true justice, but at least you and other families will know the truth. Maybe that will bring everyone some measure of peace."

CHAPTER TWENTY-TWO

*J*anet arrived at the Culinary Arts room winded and sweaty after power-walking from the parking lot. It didn't help that she carried a box filled with half pints of homemade strawberry jam from a canning day with her mother back in June.

Bethany met her outside the classroom and whisked the box out of Janet's arms. "Mrs. Shaw, I am so sorry." She stood between Janet and the door, her eyes glistening.

"What? You don't have anything to be sorry for."

"Yes, I do. I told Pops about translating that letter. He got upset and said he planned to talk to you about what is and isn't appropriate, and I realized I had no right to mention that letter to anyone. I totally messed up by breaking confidentiality."

"Oh, honey." Janet took the box back out of Bethany's arms. "I'm the one who should apologize for putting you in that situation. I didn't tell you to keep the letter a secret, so you didn't break confidentiality. I do appreciate your being sensitive to that though."

"Did Pops have a complete fit? He has been kind of—I don't know. Not himself."

"I wouldn't call it a fit. He came into the café upset, but we talked it out."

Bethany peered into Janet's face. "So you're good?"

"Yes. I'm fine. Thank you for checking in."

Bethany gave Janet's arm a little pat as if she were the adult and Janet the thirteen-year-old. "Okay. I'm glad. I've been so worried."

"Everything is fine. Go ahead and join your friends."

Inside the room, Janet set her box of jam on the table and gathered her thoughts for the short presentation she had planned. Tips on preparing for the contest. Then she would send a jar of strawberry jam home with Miranda and each student.

But after her encounter with Bethany, Janet felt more determined than ever to find out the reason behind Rodd's strange behavior.

Later in the evening, Janet sat with Ian on the sofa, watching the news. Ranger cuddled on her lap while Laddie gave her a pitiful stare from beside the coffee table. "Don't worry, Laddie, I love you just as much."

Ian shut off the TV. "Now that we know the world is still in danger of flying off its axis, how was your day, love?"

Janet stroked Ranger's back and enjoyed the gentle crescendo of his purring. "Laney and I had a nice visit with Ray today. We told him about Jonas."

"How did he take it?"

"He was rattled, understandably. But it also brought him relief to know his friend didn't die in the war after all, and had a long, happy life filled with love. That's all Ray ever wanted for him. His biggest regret was that Jonas went through the frightening experience of finding that letter alone, and that he couldn't help Jonas by convincing him to go to the police. He said Jonas told him before they left for basic training that his father might be in trouble."

Laddie wandered over to Ian, who indulged him with a scratch between the ears. "I know, Laddie. You are so neglected." He reached under the coffee table for a rubber newspaper toy and tossed it for Laddie, who scampered after it. "I'm sure that even eighty years ago, the Dennison Police Department would have taken that letter seriously."

"From what we read in Edda's replies to his letters, I think he was trying to protect Gracie, and possibly also his parents' memory. He was probably afraid of how people would see his father if they found out he'd gotten in deep with someone like that."

"I'm not sure what good it will do, but maybe I can take a look at the letter. If Laney doesn't mind."

"I'm sure she'll be grateful for your input. I'll send her a text." She moved Ranger off her lap and went to the kitchen to retrieve her phone from the charger. She sent a quick text and got an almost immediate reply. "Laney is going to take a picture of the letter right now and send it to me."

A moment later, Janet's phone pinged again with an image of the decades-old, typed letter.

Janet texted, THANKS! Then she forwarded the image to Ian and returned her phone to its charger. "Did that come through all right?" she called.

"Got it." Moments later, Ian joined Janet in the kitchen.

Janet leaned against the kitchen counter, folding her arms over her chest. "On another note, I got a visit from Rodd Nickles today.

He confronted me at the café over asking Bethany to translate Laney's letter."

Ian frowned. "That doesn't sound like something Rodd would do. I thought her parents were okay with it."

"They were. But the way Rodd behaved, you'd think I had hired his granddaughter to do something illegal. I wonder if Bethany's parents got the same lecture I did." She repeated Rodd's comment about leaving the past alone. "Do you find it strange that he also got mad when Christine wanted to investigate the history of the Townsend house to prove the Farrells were liars, and told Laney she should let her curiosity about her grandfather's connection to the house go?"

Ian opened the dishwasher and started loading the dinner dishes from the sink. "What the pattern tells me is that he fears having something related to the house uncovered. I wonder what it is."

"Well, we know Rodd couldn't have been the guy who threatened Jonas." Janet rinsed a dish and handed it to Ian. "That person would have to be at least Ray's age by now."

Ian placed the plate on the bottom rack of the dishwasher. "He's too young to be the one who left the note. But he's not too young to know who did write it."

Janet mulled over her conversation with Ian the next morning while kneading dough for cinnamon bread. If Rodd knew who had threatened Jonas, why not speak up? Even if the person was, say, a relative, Rodd wouldn't face repercussions for their crimes. Then again, maybe he was trying to protect his family's reputation too.

Janet's parents had always reminded her, "The truth comes out eventually." They were such proponents of honesty that the few times she'd fibbed or left out part of a story for fear of consequences, she got in more trouble for lying than for the original offense.

What about Bethany and Rodd's other grandkids? *He probably thinks he's protecting them.* But if his history included some unflattering secrets, wouldn't it be better for them to hear the truth from their grandfather, who had obviously chosen a very different path than whomever he was ashamed of in his family line, than online or from kids at school? Bethany was not only an intelligent girl, but also insightful and kind. If she knew her grandfather was afraid to share something from his family's past, she would be the first to reassure him. Janet felt certain of it.

When Debbie arrived at the café, Janet gave her the highlights of the afternoon and evening, from the moment she and Laney told Ray about Jonas to her conversation with Ian. "Now that we know the story behind how Laney ended up with a picture of a fallen soldier's family home, I am determined to get to the bottom of what really happened to Jonas's parents. Even if it means letting something surface that Rodd Nickles is trying to keep under wraps."

"I never suspected that you would let it go while there were still things to be unraveled." Debbie sniffed the air. "I love it when you make cinnamon bread. Fall may not be in the air yet, but the fragrance is." She pulled a stool over to Janet's work area. "Remember that story Patricia told us about the example from one of her law school courses? The one that a professor used in a discussion about circumstantial evidence."

Janet checked her rising cinnamon bread and set the oven to preheat. "That's right. The man who died in a suspicious gas leak lived in Uhrichsville. He might as well have lived in Dennison." After a week of reading letters and speculating about the circumstances that brought Abe Halner into existence, Patricia's illustration took on a new level of relevance.

"You found an article about a crime ring in Dennison, and Rodd is worried about some secret connected with the Townsend house. I'm beginning to suspect some kind of connection."

"Me too, now that I'm no longer staring at a pile of old letters," Janet said.

"And that would make Rodd's reluctance completely understandable."

An hour and a half later, Debbie served Patricia her daily peppermint mocha and Janet came out of the kitchen with a fresh slice of buttered cinnamon bread. She let Patricia take a few sips of her mocha and savor half of her cinnamon bread before swooping in.

She began with the news about Jonas Townsend surviving the war but fleeing town.

"Are you kidding me? That's incredible. Does my grandpa know?"

"I'm sure we'll find out as soon as he shows up this morning. Laney and I told Ray yesterday." Janet wasn't sure whether Ray would have told his old friend, but she was more curious about something else at the moment. "Patricia, I've thinking about that story you told me and Debbie the other day, about that example of circumstantial evidence that came up in one of your law school courses."

Patricia stirred her mocha. "The man who was suspected of murder but couldn't be found guilty?"

"That's the one."

Debbie added FRESH CINNAMON BREAD to the special board. "What did you say his name was?"

"Clive Baringer. But that was an alias. He and several accomplices were arrested right here in Dennison, at a shoe repair shop of all places. They had an illegal gambling room in back."

Janet made a mental note to send that detail to Laney as soon as she knew more. "Jonas Townsend's father tried to launch a mechanic shop. Did the professor include any of the accomplices in the discussion?"

"No, but he did include one of the other aliases. I only remember because it caused such a disruption. It was J.R. Knuckles."

Janet caught herself fighting back a laugh. "I'm sorry. I know this isn't a funny thing at all. But J.R. Knuckles sounds like a cartoon character."

Patricia put down her mug. "That's exactly how the class reacted. I wish I had a video of Professor Cohn saying 'J.R. Knuckles' as deadpan and serious as he had when saying 'Clive Baringer,' while the whole class sat there choking on our laughter. Professor Cohn actually reprimanded a student for laughing. 'Young man,' he said, 'do you plan to laugh when questioning a witness who happens to have a name that you find humorous?'"

Janet made a big production out of replacing her laugh with a stern frown and straightening her back to be as rigid as possible. "I wonder whatever became of Mr. Knuckles." On the inside, she willed herself not to appear too eager. She also didn't want to mention Rodd Nickles's role in her search for information.

Debbie pulled her phone out of her apron pocket. "Let's see what we can find out." She slipped onto the stool beside Patricia, and her thumbs flew across her screen. "Janet, listen to this. J.R. Knuckles is on a list called 'Getting Away with Murder: Notorious Criminals Who Did.'"

Patricia leaned closer to Debbie. "Yep. That's him. I remember that sleek hair and waxed mustache from a slide our professor showed us."

Debbie enlarged her screen with her fingertips and read aloud, "'J.R. Knuckles, also known as Clive Baringer and the Mechanic, was suspected in over half a dozen suspicious deaths in the Dennison, Ohio, area between 1940 and 1952, when he died in prison while serving a sentence for money laundering, bank fraud, illegal gambling, and assault. Knuckles was born Horace James Nickles in—'" Debbie stopped abruptly. "I think you're onto something, Janet."

Patricia leaned back on her stool. "Did you say Nickles? Keep reading. I'm in suspense now."

The café was still empty except for Patricia, so Janet decided to fill her in. She might be able to help, and if anyone understood discretion, it was the lawyer. "This is speculation at this point, so please keep it confidential."

"You have my word. And just so you know, I recognize the last name too. As far as I know, only one Nickles family lives in Dennison. But it wouldn't hurt to check."

Janet reached into the pocket of her sweatshirt for her phone. "I'll find out right now." She entered *Nickles Dennison Uhrichsville*

Ohio. "At first glance, I see a coin-collecting club called Save Your Nickels, an online shop called Nickeled and Dimed where you can buy jewelry made from old coins, and Rodrick Nickles, Real Estate."

Debbie went back to reading the article. "'Nickles earned the nickname Knuckles in high school because of his reputation for getting into fistfights.'" She wrinkled her nose. "How original. 'According to a confession from an accomplice shortly after Nickles' death, Nickles became known in Ohio crime rings as the Mechanic because of his habit of tampering with cars, motorcycles, delivery trucks, and even a police car owned by individuals who ended up on the List, often because of large gambling debts or unpaid loans.' He kept a list of people he might kill? Yikes," Debbie said. "These crimes happened decades ago, and Rodd didn't commit any of them. But if I were related to this person, I might want to keep it private too."

"But now that we know why Jonas Townsend left Dennison, it's time for the whole story to come to light for the sake of those who knew and loved him," Janet said. "Rodd is the one person I know of who can make that happen."

She saw Harry and Crosby through the café window and put her phone away to give them her full attention. "Let's put this on hold for now."

Debbie went back to the specials board. "Hey, Patricia. Give me your lawyerly opinion. Should we offer soup and salad with a roll for the lunch special today, or the burger with choice of fries or onion rings?"

Patricia laughed. "In my lawyerly opinion, definitely the burger."

"I completely agree." Debbie started writing.

Janet put off checking her supply of frozen onion rings until she had a chance to talk to Harry.

He came through the door with a big smile on his face. "Ray called me yesterday to share the news about Jonas Townsend."

Patricia got up from her stool and met her grandpa halfway into the dining area with a big hug. "I am so happy for you and Ray, and for Laney Farrell's family."

"After what Ray shared, I'm a mix of happy and sad. Happy that Jonas survived the war but sad for why he left Dennison. But maybe it's not too late to do what Jonas couldn't."

While waiting for slices of cinnamon bread to emerge from the toaster, Janet texted the article about Horace Nickles to Ian at the police station with a brief note. When her phone chimed again, Janet assumed it was Ian acknowledging her note, but it was Laney instead.

Are you busy this afternoon? I have something to show you.

Janet pulled up her calendar. Compared to when she still had a teenager in the house, her Friday calendar revealed a possible need for a new hobby. I'm free from 2:00 on.

Laney responded, I'm still in Barnhill with Mom. We're going to have lunch at a cute place we saw and then I'm heading back. 2:30?

Janet went to the stove and checked her pot of vegetable soup then confirmed, Perfect. How about if I meet you at the Pullman?

Great.

Janet put her phone away so it wouldn't end up in the soup. *I have something to show you too, Laney.*

Janet used the time between leaving the café and meeting Laney at the Pullman to relax in the depot and send an email to the members of the Culinary Arts Club telling them how excited she and Debbie were to host them.

She spotted Kim Smith in her ticket office and went over to check in with her about contest details.

Kim opened the side door and waved Janet in. "I'm going to show you something, but you have to promise not to tell anyone. It's a surprise for the contest."

Janet crossed her heart. "I won't say a word."

Kim pulled out a folder and handed it to Janet. "I still need to frame them."

As soon as Janet opened it, she had to clap her hand over her mouth to keep her laughter quiet. "That is one of the cutest things I have ever seen. Did you make those?"

"Yes, on one of those free design sites. I bought some fancy printer paper, and voila."

Janet returned the folder to keep Kim's surprise safe from onlookers.

"Mom is so excited that she asked me to take her shopping for a new outfit. Mom never buys new clothes. She always says, 'A woman of my age doesn't need one more thing to leave behind for her loved ones to weed through.' I told her I will not only be taking her shopping, but we're going for mani-pedis as well." Kim stashed the folder.

Janet imagined Eileen in a pedicure chair. "You better send me a picture of that."

"You'll get lots of pictures. I'm also volunteering as taxi driver for your celebrity judges the day of the contest. I scheduled one of my part-timers to cover the ticket desk."

"Thank you, Kim. That eliminates one task from my list."

"I thought of another idea as well. Do you think it would be weird to contact the *Gazette* about the baking contest? If the club is hoping to use the winner's baked good as a fundraiser, a little publicity wouldn't hurt. Even if the *Gazette* does a tiny write-up in the local events section, it'll help. I'd be happy to handle it."

"I don't think it would be weird at all. Go for it. If they pass, the kids will never know, but if they send one of their writers over, it'll be a fun surprise."

"I hoped you would say that. I'll call them right now."

Janet hugged her and made her way over to the Pullman cars. She climbed the steps to the old railcar and found Laney's compartment at the end of the row of sleeper car rooms.

Laney opened the door, her face sun-kissed and happy after the day out with her mom. "Come on in."

Janet looked around the small compartment. The Pullmans had become extremely popular, and she understood why. "These rooms are so fun. If Ian and I didn't live right here in town, I would book one for us for a weekend."

"I guess that's the downside of living in a tourist town. The visitors get to have all the fun while the locals work like always." She patted the bench seat beside a dining car-style table by a window with a view of the old tracks. "Have a seat."

Janet spotted a roller suitcase and the tote bag full of letters and items from the safe-deposit box beside the coffee station in the corner. "Are you packing to leave?"

"Yes, I need to head back to Lakewood tonight. But this isn't goodbye. It's 'see you later.' Brian and I are still very interested in the house, and I'm continuing to research what might have happened to my grandfather's parents."

Janet took out her phone. "I have something that might help you with that. Ian is looking into it too." She pulled up the article from that morning. "I'm sending it to you now."

Laney sat across from Janet and opened the link. Janet gave her a moment to read the article. "I'm reading all this and wondering how it's possible that the police didn't nail this guy. But I guess his guilt is obvious to us because we're personally invested."

"I have a lawyer friend who was explaining that they couldn't get him because all the evidence was circumstantial. I'll let you know if anything else comes out." Janet swung her feet under the table. "So, what did you find today?"

Laney tapped her phone screen. "Mom and I found the bench from the picture in Grandpa's notebook. It's in Stagecoach Park if you ever want to go there. And because of this, I think I know the reason behind Grandpa's road trips."

CHAPTER TWENTY-THREE

Abe drove until his Plymouth almost ran out of gas at a little after six o'clock in the morning. Everything with Jonas Townsend's name on it was in a small cardboard box on the passenger side of the seat. His birth certificate and social security card. His dog tags. The letter and pictures that Edda DeSmett gave him the day they said goodbye. Every letter and card she or Jean or one of the children sent after the war. Gracie's prayer tucked into his worn New Testament, and the bracelet meant for her. Even the letter demanding payment of his father's debt.

"You lied to me." Ivy's reaction still stung a week after he told her the truth. She hadn't sounded angry that night. More matter-of-fact, as if she'd shut off his emotional access to her.

He'd told her about Gracie. His parents dying in an accident. Being wounded, losing his friend Chip, and waking up on a cot in the DeSmetts' basement. Seeing his name in the newspaper, listed as Killed in Action. Coming home from the war to a letter demanding fulfillment of a debt that he couldn't pay. His reasons for keeping it from the police. Taking a bus to St. Louis. Changing his name to Abraham J. Halner with the help of the obituary section of a newspaper.

"Why did you wait so long to tell me?"

He had been afraid of losing her, but that wasn't a good enough reason.

"I need time to think."

How could he blame her?

He would need to think too after hearing all he'd shared. Even while telling her the whole truth, he had been struck by the heaviness of his own story, as if he was talking about someone else's experiences. But all of it had happened to him. I used to be Jonas Townsend. *Now that boy felt less and less like him every day but also refused to let go altogether.*

Abe tried to pray as he drove. God, I love Ivy. *He'd never expected to love anyone as much as he'd loved Gracie, but he did.* I don't want to lose her after all I've lost already.

He didn't even know where he was headed, only that every mile took him a little closer to Dennison. The town he dared not enter again, yet where he most longed to be.

Abe finally exited the highway in Barnhill and found a parking lot in front of a diner and a credit union. He closed his eyes and prayed some more. God, I thought becoming someone else would make things easier, but sometimes I still feel torn between two worlds—my old life as Jonas and my new life as Abe.

He had a job at a car dealership, a small apartment, and was taking night classes toward an engineering degree at the community college. But he still caught himself watching over his shoulder for a strange man introducing himself as C.B.

Meeting Ivy at the potluck at Eastside Community Church had felt like waking up from a long, sad dream. He was a first-time visitor when a couple in the pew behind his insisted he stay for the fellowship lunch.

He was having a hard time deciding what he wanted for dessert after so many months of living off canned food and diner specials.

A beautiful dark-haired woman behind him had said, "I made the apple pie."

So that was what he'd picked. After the first bite, he'd also chosen to ask her on a date.

Four months had passed since that day. Four months of movies and walks and talking well into the night.

He glanced over at the box again. What am I doing here? It was too late to go to the police about his parents' accident and too late to undo falling in love with Ivy.

Whether she takes me back or not, I need to decide who I am. Jonas Townsend, who is on the run, or Abe Halner, who has a happy, stable life.

The diner beside the credit union was open, offering a special of ham, steak, and eggs for seventy-five cents. Maybe it would help to eat something and figure out what to do next. Or why he'd come all this way with a box full of memories and the firm conviction that letting go of those things might make his life as Abe Halner a bit lighter.

On the way into the diner, he saw a sign in the window of Capital Members Bank advertising the prices for safe-deposit boxes.

Jonas would be safe there.

What a strange thought.

Abe stood over a crack in the sidewalk between the diner and Capital Members Bank. He looked at his watch then back at the sign. Capital Members Bank opened in thirty minutes. So he went into the diner for the special and a cup of coffee to consider his idea and examine his budget. He made pretty good money *selling cars at the dealership, but his night classes ate into his precious funds. Other students who'd fought in the war had their tuition paid for by the G.I. Bill. But as a veteran classified as KIA, he had to pay his own tuition.*

Abe added the cost of a small safe-deposit box to his monthly expenses.

If I spend less on groceries and entertainment, I can do it.

I must do it.

The sun was setting when he opened the door of his apartment in St. Louis, with the key to a Capital Members Bank safe-deposit box tucked into one of the slots in his wallet. Without Jonas's identification documents and letters and Gracie's bracelet, he felt more like Abe Halner. Less haunted by all that brought him to St. Louis. Like if a strange man tapped him on the shoulder and said, "Jonas, I've been looking for you," he could say, "Sorry, you have the wrong guy."

He collapsed onto his bed and slept all night in his clothes and without covers. He woke to the sound of his phone ringing from his nightstand.

He jolted upright. Did I sleep through work?

He checked his clock and sank back against his pillow. It was almost nine o'clock, and he didn't have to be at work until noon.

He rolled over on his side and fumbled for the phone receiver. "Hello?"

"Hi, Abe." It was Ivy. "Sorry to call so early, but can I come over?"

He sat up and ran his hands through his rumpled hair. "Of course."

He cleaned up and changed as quickly as he could. Whatever Ivy had to say, he didn't want to look like a mess. By the time she rang his doorbell, Abe had coffee brewing and was finishing a piece of buttered toast.

She stood on his welcome mat wearing a necklace he'd given her. That felt like a good sign.

"Come in." Abe held the door open for Ivy and pulled out a chair for her at his kitchen table. "Can I offer you some breakfast?"

"No thank you. I just ate."

When she didn't sit in the chair, Abe's heart sank a little.

"Abe, I'm done thinking."

He told himself not to jump to conclusions. No matter what she said, he would not let it be the end of the world. He had a whole life ahead of him as Abe Halner. "And?"

*"And it upset me a lot to know you'd been keep-
ing secrets from me. That you'd been living a double
life. But last night, I couldn't sleep. Not a wink. I
kept thinking about everything you told me. When my
brother-in-law came home from fighting in the Pacific,
he had a family waiting. You didn't have anyone except
Gracie. Then you had to leave her behind too. I was so
sad for you."* She sounded like she had a lump in her
throat. She cleared it and went on. *"You could have
given up after all you went through. You could have
become bitter and hard, shutting out everyone around
you. But you didn't. You rebuilt your life. You're going
to college and paying for it yourself. You told me everything even though you didn't know how I would react.
You are a very brave, strong person, Abe."*

*"I never thought of it as brave. I was doing what-
ever I could to escape whoever sent that letter."*

*"But it was brave. I realized I love you. I don't
care what your name is. I know who you are, which is
more important."* She wiped away a tear, even as his
heart soared. *"Plus, you know, you could still go to
the police."*

*How many times he had considered doing that
only to consider what it would mean—possible justice
for his parents but also the black mark of gambling
and running from a bookie on his father's memory.*

Even if C.B.—whoever he was—went to prison, he most likely had friends who would remain free and search for Abe.

"Ivy, the man who sent that letter rigged my parents' car so it would crash. I don't have proof, but I know it in my heart. It's too big a risk. Besides, it's been so long that the police probably can't do anything anyway."

"Well, if you ever change your mind, I'll go with you."

He gaped at her. "You would do that?"

"Yes, I would." Ivy took his hands. "I don't ever want you to have to face something painful and hard alone again. In the meantime, your secret is safe with me."

Abe wrapped his arms around Ivy and drew her close. "Thank you." Thank You, God.

Ivy kissed Abe's cheek. "We're in this together."

He took her hands again. "I drove to Ohio yesterday. To a town called Barnhill, outside Dennison."

Ivy led Abe over to the table and sat in the chair he pulled out for her. "You drove all that way and back in one day?"

Abe scooted the other chair close to Ivy. "I needed to think." He told her about the safe-deposit box and all he'd left behind in it.

"You didn't need to do that. Jonas Townsend will always be part of who you are. I don't want you to think my keeping your secret must include you never talking about your old life again."

"That isn't why I did it. I felt like it was time to live my life as Abe. Even the DeSmetts know me as Abe now. As soon as I can, I'm going to change my name legally."

"I hope you won't stop writing to them. They're your friends."

"You wouldn't mind?"

"No. You don't expect me to stop communicating with friends I knew before meeting you, do you? The DeSmetts took care of you. I know this is a big request, but I want to meet them someday."

Tears spilled down Abe's cheeks in a way that hadn't happened since Gracie told him about his parents' accident. But this time, they weren't from grief.

"Oh, I'm sorry, sweetheart. What's wrong? Was it something I said?" Ivy got up and wrapped her arms around him.

"I'm not sad. I'm so thankful that I haven't lost you."

"You haven't. And I meant what I said about the police. If you ever decide to report what happened, you won't have to do it alone."

"If I do, it'll be to find out who caused my parents' accident. But I'm afraid it might even be too late for that."

Ivy let go and pulled a chair close to Abe's. "Last night when I couldn't sleep, it hit me that you never had a service for your mom and dad."

"No. I planned to, after the war, but circumstances prevented it."

"I know it's too late to have one at a cemetery, but we could figure out another way to honor them."

Abe took hold of Ivy's hands and felt his tears drying on his eyelashes. "I would like that. Someday, I want to be able to buy a plaque or something."

"Yes. We'll place it somewhere they would like. Maybe a park where you can go and remember them. Honoring your parents is one thing it's not too late for."

CHAPTER TWENTY-FOUR

*L*aney tapped her phone screen and held out a much clearer image of the park bench from her grandfather's notebook.

Janet scrolled through other pictures of the bench from creative angles, two of Laney sitting on it, one of Laney's mom, and some close-ups of a memorial plaque on the back, dedicated to Larry and Bridget Townsend in September 1953. "This is beautiful."

"Mom and I sat there reading through some of Edda's letters. Edda even wrote to Grandma Ivy after they met in 1960. We found a letter that Mila wrote after Edda died, in 1994, and we both cried."

Janet felt an unexpected sadness. Logically, she had assumed Edda would be gone, but the confirmation still stung somehow. "I can understand why you would. I feel like I knew her, and she isn't even connected to my family."

"That's exactly it. She feels like family. So do her kids. Jean passed in 2010."

Janet handed Laney's phone back to her. "What about Mila and Oskar? If they're still living, they would probably like to know about your grandpa."

"That's another thing that happened today. Mom and I noticed that the letters tapered off quite a bit after Edda died. But we do know that Oskar moved to the States after college and married an

American woman, and Mila ended up in Paris teaching art. During lunch, Mom and I searched Oskar DeSmett's name for the fun of it and found him on social media. He lives in Columbus now. I sent him a message and attached a picture of a letter from his mother, so he knows I'm not a troll."

"Laney, I'm so happy for you. Let me know if you hear back from him."

"You bet." Laney set her phone down and gazed toward her suitcase and bag of memories. "When I get home, I'm going to buy a nice box to store all the letters and the rest of the things I found. Something that will protect them for years to come."

"I bet you could even find something with a military theme."

"That's what I'm hoping. And if I do connect with Oskar and that leads to meeting Mila, I wonder if it might be nice for me to give her the fleur-de-lis bracelet, to return it to the family. I can tell it's high quality. I saw a stamp on the back of the charm that says it's eighteen-karat gold."

"I don't think Mila or Oskar would expect you to do that. It was a gift to your grandfather from their mother. You can always offer, but I think they would want you to keep it. And if your grandfather left a key for the safe-deposit box, he wanted you to have the contents. Including the bracelet."

Laney got up from the table and reached into the tote bag to retrieve the velvet jewelry box. "You think so?"

"I'm sure of it. You came to Dennison looking for a house and spent the better part of two weeks here trying to get to know the person who'd left a picture of it. That if nothing else will tell them what kind of person you are."

Laney opened the box and took out the bracelet. "I sure didn't expect what I found. But I'm so glad I did." She unclipped the clasp. "Will you help me put this on?"

"Of course." Janet secured the bracelet around her friend's wrist. "Whatever happens with the information we've found, or with the house, your family knows the real Abe Halner, and Ray finally knows what happened to his friend."

Midway through a steady Saturday morning at the café, Janet went out to the dining area to check her supply of baked goods and help Debbie prepare for the lunch rush.

Debbie met her at the counter with a tray of empty juice glasses and coffee mugs. "I'm going to miss seeing Laney around here."

Janet took an order pad and pen out of her apron pocket to jot down what needed replenishing. "She promised to keep in touch and to stop in next time she and Brian come to Dennison, which I imagine will happen once the Townsend house finally goes up for sale." She wrote *morning buns, cinnamon rolls, cranberry scones.* "Laney heard from Oskar DeSmett last night, and she and Brian are planning a time to meet him in Columbus for a visit. I expect to get a full report on how that goes too."

"Wonderful. You'll share that with me, right?" Debbie started toward the kitchen with her tray.

"You bet." Janet tore her list off the order pad and began to follow, but stopped when the café door opened with a welcoming jingle.

Christine Murray approached the counter.

Janet kept her voice bright. "Good morning, Christine. What can I get for you?"

Christine set her purse on the counter and folded her hands on top of it. "Can we talk? Just you and me?"

"Sure."

Debbie came out of the kitchen and took Janet's list from her. "I'll refill the bakery case. Go ahead and take a break while it's slow."

After a week of discoveries, whatever Christine might have to say suddenly felt manageable. Janet was happy to let the answers come to her for once. "How about if we go outside and take a walk?"

Christine swung her purse over her shoulder again. "That would be lovely."

They walked out into the entryway. "What can I do for you?" Janet asked.

Christine took a deep breath. "Janet, I owe you an apology. It was out of line for me to come storming into your place of business with my assumptions about Laney and Brian."

"You're forgiven, Christine. We were all excited about your idea for the Dennison House. I can see why you would be upset over someone else wanting the same house you had in mind."

"I fully flipped out, and it was unprofessional. I sent an apology to the chamber of commerce, Rodd, and the Graysons as well. I was about to reach out to Laney and Brian when Laney sent an email to me." Christine stopped at the edge of the platform, beside the rail lined with cutouts of servicemen. "She wanted me to know that she doesn't expect her grandfather's connection to the house to give her and Brian special favor with Chad and Theresa."

"See. You had nothing to worry about."

Christine rested her hand on the rail. "I guess a themed B and B wouldn't be the end of the world. Anything that contributes to our local economy, right? More places for people to stay overnight will bring more business to the town."

Janet leaned against the rail. "Christine, while helping Laney over the last week or so, I learned some things about Jonas Townsend. And Gracie Pike, the woman he planned to marry."

"So you found out she is my grandmother?" The way Christine said it, it wasn't really a question.

"We did. Is that why you reacted so strongly?"

Christine went over to the bench on the opposite side of the platform. She sank into it and squinted up at Janet as if an embarrassing secret had just been uncovered. "Yes. My grandmother should have spent her whole adult life there. I should have grown up with it as my home away from home."

Janet sat beside her. "You knew about her relationship with Jonas then."

Christine leaned her head back against the wall of the depot. "Nanny told me about her first love, Jonas Townsend, when I was fifteen. My first boyfriend had broken up with me right before the winter formal. My sister and I were staying with Nanny and Papa while our parents were out of town. I could not stop crying that night. Nanny sat next to me on the bed in her guest room and rubbed my back, letting me cry. After a few minutes, she said, 'I know how you feel, sweetie. I remember a time when I thought I would never be happy again.' Then she told me about Jonas going off to war, and a game they played where they pretended that he was going on a school trip. She told me about when his parents died, and she had to be the one to tell Jonas in a letter. Then she saw his name in a list of soldiers who'd been killed in action. She was so devastated that she went to live with her sister for eight months."

Janet felt a jolt in her stomach. "What a horrible way to receive that news. I thought the army would have sent her a telegram or something."

Christine shook her head. "They weren't married and he had no surviving relatives, so officially he didn't have a next of kin. One of her letters was found in the pocket of Jonas's overcoat, along with an unmailed letter to her, already addressed. The army was kind enough to send them to her. She kept them even after she met and married Papa. She showed them to me that night when she comforted me."

The thought of such a young woman receiving such mail made Janet's heart ache.

"After that, we went to the kitchen and drank hot cocoa. I remember thinking that what she went through was so much worse than a breakup before a dance. She had lost the man she planned to marry. But she didn't compare her loss to mine. Instead, she told me about meeting Papa at a community dance. 'You'll find someone, Christine. You are smart, pretty, and a real go-getter. Who wouldn't fall in love with that?' I never did find the one, but I appreciate what she was doing." She idly ran a hand over the bench. "Every time I saw the Townsend house after that, I thought of Nanny's story about Jonas. She loved Papa, but I still wanted to honor her love for Jonas."

Christine's eyes filled, and she gave Janet a sad smile. "Now I know that Jonas was alive the whole time and living as Abe Halner. Laney told me in her email. It breaks my heart that Nanny will never know."

Janet scooted a little closer to Christine. "He left everything behind to keep her safe. Her and his parents' memories. He must have really loved her."

"I wish Nanny were still alive so I could tell her." She slowly drummed her fingers on the side of her purse. "Or maybe it's better this way. If it's confusing for me, I can't imagine how she would feel. Gracie had a wonderful life with Papa Glen, and I wouldn't be here without that."

"Based on what I learned about Laney's grandfather, Jonas would be very happy to know Gracie had a beautiful life." Janet met Christine's gaze and smiled. "And he would be excited about all you've done for the Dennison Preservation Society."

"He might even think he had a little part in that." She rose from the bench. "No matter who gets the house, it's nice to know that we'll always have a little bit of a good man like Jonas Townsend in Dennison."

CHAPTER TWENTY-FIVE

*A*fter closing the café on Monday afternoon, Janet and Debbie cleared a table to make a sign for the baking contest, using the biggest poster board Janet could find.

She opened a flat plastic bin from Tiffany's years of doing school projects. "I found permanent markers, decorative tape, glitter stars, and stencils for writing."

"And I found these." Debbie showed her a packet of large baking-themed stickers—cartoony chefs, cupcakes with fancy frosting, cookies, and smiling utensils with arms and legs.

"Where did you get those?"

"Online." Debbie opened the packet. "Should we use the stickers as a border, or use the tape and save the stickers for after we do the lettering?"

Janet checked her tape options. "I have butterflies, blue stripes, and red-and-white polka dots. So how about the stripes along the top and bottom, polka dots on the sides, and random stickers throughout?"

Debbie took a pencil out of the art supplies container. Janet was about to pull the stencils they would need when her phone rang.

"Hang on, it's my husband." She handed the stencil letters to Debbie and answered the call. "Hey, handsome."

"Hello, love. Do we have anything on the calendar tonight that I may have forgotten about?"

"I don't think so. Debbie and I are making a sign for the contest right now, but the evening is free. Why? What's up?"

"I know this is very last-minute, but Rodd Nickles wants to meet with us tonight. He didn't say why, but after our discussion and the article you sent, I have a feeling I know."

Janet watched Debbie create a perfectly straight line of striped tape at the top of the sign. "Sure. Should we invite him to our house, maybe after dinner? I can bring some leftover cookies home as dessert."

"Sounds good. Thanks, hon. Sorry to throw this at you on such short notice."

"If it's about what you think, it'll be worth it." Janet witnessed the placement of another exquisite line of tape and gave Debbie a thumbs-up.

"Rodd was hoping to include Laney and Brian as well, but they've left town already."

"I'll text Laney. Maybe they can join us on video."

"If you can make that happen, I'm sure Rodd will appreciate it. He sounded eager to talk to all of us."

Janet ended her call with Ian as Debbie finished the tape border. "Well, that was interesting. Rodd Nickles wants to talk to me and Ian tonight, and hopefully the Farrells too." She pulled up Laney's number and started a text. "I'm going to see if Laney and Brian can call in." She sent the message then went back to sorting letters for the sign.

At last, Janet held up a fun, colorful sign, speckled with stars and baking stickers clustered in the corners. While Debbie found a place to store it until Saturday's contest, Janet checked her phone and found a reply from Laney.

BRIAN HAS A MEETING, BUT I AM VERY INTERESTED IN HEARING WHAT RODD HAS TO SAY. INSTEAD OF A VIDEO CALL, HOW ABOUT IF I COME OVER? I FEEL LIKE I SHOULD HEAR RODD'S NEWS IN PERSON.

Janet sent up a quick prayer. *Lord, please let Rodd's news be worth the trip for Laney.*

After dinner, Laney arranged a dozen peanut butter cookies on a plate. The fleur-de-lis bracelet sparkled on her wrist. "Thanks for inviting me to spend the night, Janet. I hope I'm not putting you out."

"Not at all. Tiffany's room is empty, and if this talk with Rodd gets tense or upsetting, I don't want you driving back to Lakewood by yourself."

The doorbell rang. Laney jumped.

Janet squeezed her shoulder. "Don't worry. It'll be fine."

"Thanks. I'm sure you're right." Laney took the cookies into the dining room.

Janet started a pot of decaf coffee and tried to predict why Rodd wanted to talk to them. Did he want to issue an ultimatum about bidding on the house? Or perhaps he was officially handing the Townsend house over to another Realtor.

She overheard Rodd greeting Laney and making friends with Laddie. She wiped her hands on a clean dish towel and went to the dining room to greet Rodd with her most hospitable smile. Ian already sat at the table.

"Hi, Janet. I appreciate the three of you meeting me." Rodd set a folder on the table.

Laney took a seat. "I'm eager to hear what you have to say."

"Have a seat," Ian offered.

Rodd did. Janet noticed that his defensive demeanor was gone, replaced by a palpable nervousness. "Before I share what I have to say, Janet, I want to apologize for storming into the café and speaking to you the way I did. The sale of the Townsend house has opened a wound, as they say. But it's one that needed to be dealt with." He tapped the folder on the table. "Mrs. Farrell, I understand that your grandfather, Abe Halner, also known as Jonas Townsend, lost his parents in a car accident."

"Yes." Laney toyed with her bracelet.

"Well, I happen to know that there was nothing accidental about it." He held up the folder. "When I was about ten, I needed information about both sets of grandparents for a family tree assignment. I was a pretty independent kid, so I went poking around in the attic where I knew Mom kept old photo albums and family information. I found a box taped shut and stored in the back corner of the highest shelf. Every other box had a label—CHRISTMAS ORNAMENTS, BABY BOOKS & TOYS, TAX RETURNS—except that one, which of course sparked curiosity. So I opened it."

He paused, clearly considering what to say next, and Janet fought the urge to prompt him to continue.

When he did, his words surprised her. "I'd always wondered why my dad never talked about his father, other than telling me he wouldn't win Father of the Year and that his parents divorced when he was a baby."

Janet noticed the tension in Rodd's hands. "May I offer you some refreshments?"

"No, thanks. I need to get this out." He cleared his throat. "Long story short, I found out that my grandfather died in prison in the early fifties. He was there for extortion- and gambling-related crimes. But according to what I found in that box in the attic, he was guilty of a lot more than that. Including murder." He held the folder out to Ian. "This folder contains a list of names. People who owed my grandfather, Horace Nickles, money. Gambling debts, business loans, loans taken out in pure desperation. It includes photos of their vehicles, their homes, and notes of possible 'accidents.'"

Laney lowered her forehead onto her hand, exhaling shakily.

"Laney, I also wanted you to know that if you read or heard anything about your grandfather's father owing a gambling debt, it was likely false. Horace Nickles had a pattern of granting business loans and then including an attractive offer of a lower interest rate if the borrower allowed him to use the building during off-hours."

"For gambling purposes?" Laney asked.

"Yes. Then, if the borrower found out what was going on and wanted out of the deal, Horace started making threats, jacked up their interest rates, and even added false gambling debts to their files."

Janet's jaw dropped. "That's horrible."

Rodd's voice tightened. "I'm so sorry, Laney, but I am certain that my grandfather caused Larry and Bridget Townsend's car accident."

Janet saw that Laney was on the verge of tears and put an arm around her shoulders. "Laney and I found a threatening letter. It had been left for Jonas when he came home from the war, demanding that he pay his father's debt with interest."

"I have no doubt that my grandfather left that. Based on what I've learned over the years, it's the sort of thing he would do. I am truly sorry, both for your family's loss and for wanting to keep the truth hidden."

Laney lifted her head. "What Horace Nickles did isn't your fault. I'm upset for my grandfather—what he went through and the burden he had to carry. But I don't blame you."

Janet watched Rodd's eyes fill with tears. "I appreciate that. I really do. But after finding that box in the attic, I contributed to my parents' efforts to keep the story hidden. As Ian pointed out when I asked to meet, by bringing the truth to light, I can help people like you let go of lies about their loved ones. I wish Jonas Townsend could be at this table to hear that his father did not gamble, and most likely lost his auto repair business because of my grandfather's crooked lending practices." He pushed the folder toward Ian. "I want the truth of what Horace Nickles did to go on record. I sat my whole family down, grandkids and all, and told them everything, so if the story ends up public, they'll be prepared."

Ian took the folder from Rodd. "I want you to know that I plan to only use the contents of this folder for clearing up the facts in police records. I won't take it to the press."

"I appreciate that."

Janet moved her arm away from Laney's shoulders and handed her a napkin for her eyes. "And as far as I'm concerned, you will always be a respected, valuable member of this community. You are not responsible for your grandfather's sins."

Laney wiped her eyes then reached across the table and took Rodd's hand. "I am positive that my grandfather would tell you it's time to let the past rest. Thank you for doing what he couldn't and erasing the mark on Larry Townsend's legacy."

CHAPTER TWENTY-SIX

When the day of the contest arrived, Janet poured every ounce of enthusiasm into making the afternoon an experience that the Culinary Arts Club could be proud of and their guest judges would treasure. After lunch, she took out the USE IT UP, WEAR IT OUT apron that she had ordered especially for the contest. She got the sign from inside the pantry and then the number cards and checked cupcake liners from inside her tote bag.

Debbie met Janet beside the cash register. "So, I have a question. You have fifteen students and three judges. How are you going to prevent Ray, Harry, and Eileen from having a sugar crash after the contest?"

Janet held up the cupcake liners. "That, my friend, is what these are for. Miranda and I talked about it, and each contestant will bring a plate of their treats so it can be judged for appearance plus a bite-size amount for each judge."

"You did think of everything."

By closing time, Greg had set up the tables in front of the café and hung the sign. All the entries were lined up and numbered on the table closest to the café door. The judging table was set with score-cards, pencils, and water and soda crackers to cleanse the judges' palates between tastings. The depot was already abuzz with middle schoolers and their families. Janet spotted Chad and Theresa Grayson in back, and Rodd and his wife a few feet away from them.

When Kim arrived pushing Ray's chair, with her mother dressed in a brand-new salmon-pink dress, Harry in a sharp navy blue blazer and matching tie, and Crosby wearing a bow tie on his collar, the whole place erupted with applause.

Eileen laughed. "I feel like a movie star."

Janet pulled out a chair for her at the judging table. "Today, all three of you are celebrity judges."

Julian led another round of cheers and whistles.

Janet raised her hands and waited for the crowd to fall quiet. "Can I have your attention? I want to welcome you to The Dennison Middle School Culinary Arts Club Rationing Baking Contest, with our panel of experts, Eileen Palmer, Raymond Zink, and Harry Franklin."

Ray and Eileen waved. Harry stood up and took a bow.

She was halfway through introducing the students when the depot entrance opened and a woman with a camera came in, along with a young man. Kim went over to talk to them then came up front.

She whispered in Janet's ear, "They're from the newspaper. Act natural."

This is just the best. "Now, I'd like to introduce Miranda Sloan, the Culinary Arts teacher, who will explain the rules."

Miranda stepped up, wearing a 1940s-style dress. "Thank you so much for taking time out of your busy Saturday to support this project. Each student was challenged to create their own version of a World War II-era baked treat using ingredients that a family could buy with rationing coupons. As you can see, the entries are numbered, so the judges have no idea who made what. The winning entry will be for sale in the Whistle Stop Café, with proceeds going to support the Culinary Arts Club."

Janet examined the long row of cakes, custards, pies, cookies, and turnovers. "Okay, let's start the judging." She started with a baked rice pudding topped with cinnamon, setting it before the judges, along with the bite-size portions for them to eat.

The door opened again, and in walked Laney and Brian. Janet waved to them, and they waved back.

One by one, she and Debbie delivered bites to Eileen, Ray, and Harry, who made a big production out of tasting, chewing, and filling out their score sheets without giving anything away.

After the last entry had been cleared, Janet approached the judging table. "Okay, it's time for our experts to hand in their scores. While Debbie and Mrs. Sloan tally them, enjoy a few minutes to visit."

As the low murmur of conversation began, Janet seized the chance to say hello to Laney and Brian. "I didn't know you two were planning to come out for this."

Laney took hold of Brian's arm. "After hearing about it while I was here, I didn't want to miss it. I was also hoping to talk to Ray. I have something for him."

"Isn't he cute up there?"

Brian held up his phone. "We've been taking pictures."

Debbie called everyone to attention again. "Ladies and gentlemen, we are ready to announce the winner and runner-up. But first, Kim Smith has an announcement to make."

Kim hurried up front with a stack of frames in her hands. "I have a little thank-you gift for our judges. Eileen, Ray, Harry, it is my privilege to present each of you with the I Survived Sugar Rationing Award."

All three burst out laughing when Kim held up their framed certificates, which had their pictures right smack in the center of a forties-style ad motif.

Eileen took hers. "I'm hanging this on my wall at Good Shepherd. The nurses will love it."

The woman from the *Gazette* snapped a series of shots with her camera.

Kim took a step back. "Now Janet can announce the winners."

Miranda joined Janet, holding the gift cards in red boxes tied with big bows.

Janet took one of the boxes from her. "First, our runner-up will receive a twenty-five-dollar gift card, donated by Earth's Market. Who is number seven?"

Bethany raised her hand.

"Bethany Nickles, congratulations on your peanut butter and raspberry jam thumbprint cookies. The judges loved them, and personally I'd like the recipe."

Rodd shouted from the back, "Good job, Bethany!"

Bethany ran up in her soccer jersey and shorts and threw her arms around Janet. "Thank you."

Janet held out her award and held the pose for the photographer from the *Gazette*. "I'm pretty impressed by the jam on the cookies."

"Yours inspired me. It was amazing."

"Now for the top prize. I know it wasn't easy for the judges to choose, because everyone did such a great job." Janet took the other box from Miranda. "And the winner is number thirteen!"

Julian's eyes widened. He pointed to himself, staring around at his club mates as if wondering whether he'd heard the number wrong.

The kids behind him nudged him forward and cheered for him.

Janet called him up front. "Julian Connor for his apple cake with cider drizzle."

Julian high-fived his brother, Jaxon, on his way to the front, and Janet heard Jaxon tell his younger brother, "See? I told you so. It's the best cake ever."

"Here is your fifty-dollar gift card, donated by Earth's Market. I have a feeling your cake will be very popular, and might need to become a fall staple here at the Whistle Stop Café."

Julian held up his award in a victory pose.

Greg and Jaxon cheered louder than anyone else.

Janet waved her arm toward the table of baked goods. "We have plenty of goodies here. How about if our bakers pass out some samples of their masterpieces?"

The photographer raised a hand. "First, can I get a picture of the group behind the table and then the winners with their entries?"

Janet got out of the way and found Laney and Brian visiting with Rodd and Debbie.

Rodd beamed proudly at his granddaughter, posing with Julian with their awards and plates of treats. "I was telling these three that seeing Bethany up there was exactly what I needed today. It's time to stop letting what my grandfather did cast a pall over my life."

Janet watched Bethany and Julian pull Ray, Harry, and Eileen over for a picture with them. "Whenever you start to feel it creeping back in, look at that brilliant, talented granddaughter of yours. You're leaving her a legacy she can be proud of."

Rodd smiled at her. "Thank you for saying that. I'm going to go get a picture with Bethany. She'll always have first place to me."

Debbie squeezed Janet's arm. "This came out so well. Great work. I'll go slice the entries and brew some coffee. You stay here and visit."

"Do you think we can steal Ray for a few minutes?" Laney asked Janet.

Janet waited for the photographer to get a shot of Ray with smiling middle schoolers surrounding his wheelchair. "If we can drag him away from his adoring fans." She wove her way through clusters of families. "Hey, Ray. Can Laney and I borrow you for a sec?"

"Sure."

Janet waited for each student to give Ray a hug then she took the handles of his wheelchair. "Let's go outside, away from the paparazzi."

Laney held the door open, and Janet rolled Ray down the platform where he'd boarded a troop train as an eighteen-year-old in 1943. "Hey, Ray," Laney said. "Guess who Brian and I talked to the other night?"

"Who?"

"Edda DeSmett's son, Oskar. He is in his eighties and was barely five when Jonas stayed in his house, but he vividly remembers the American soldier his mother and older brother cared for. His sister is still alive, living in Paris. Oskar wants to meet you. What do you think?"

Ray's face lit up. "That would be wonderful. Let's set a date."

Laney sat on a bench and opened her tote bag. "And Ray, I have gift for you."

"You didn't need to do that."

"I wanted to. I've been thinking about your friendship with my grandfather. He wrote about you in his notebook, you know. 'R.Z. was a true friend. I could always confide in him.'" Laney reached into her tote and pulled out a square box wrapped with shiny white paper and a blue ribbon. "I know that if Jonas had stayed in Dennison after the war, you would have remained friends until the day he passed."

"We would have. I'm certain of that."

"Then I want you to have something to remember him." Laney placed the box in Ray's hand.

Ray glanced at Janet.

"I'm as clueless as you are," she told him.

Ray tugged on the ribbon and let it drop into his lap. He carefully removed the paper and opened the box. He sucked in a breath, and a few tears ran down his wrinkled cheeks. His fingers trembled as he reached into the box and took out a pair of dog tags. The chain of Jonas's tags shone from a good cleaning and polishing. He held his arm out to Laney. "Thank you. I can't tell you what this means to me."

Laney wrapped her arms around Ray's neck. "You're like family to me now. You have taught me so much."

"Now that I know your relation to Jonas, I can see that you have his smile."

"That is the biggest compliment I have received in a long time."

After Janet took Ray back to the contest crowd, she invited Laney to follow her into the café. Brian was in line at the counter with Chad and Theresa, and Debbie happily bustled around behind the counter, serving coffees.

Laney took a seat at the counter, and Janet went to take over the cash register. Everyone in the dining area seemed content with samples from Julian, Bethany, and the rest of the students.

Brian ordered an iced coffee from Debbie and sat beside his wife. "I was telling Chad and Theresa about the discoveries that came out of our search for a B and B."

Chad took out his wallet. "I am so happy for your family. My dad grew up never knowing what happened to his father, only that he fought in the Bastogne Region during the Battle of the Bulge and went missing in December 1944. So I understand how tough it can be not to know your family history, and I'm glad you got answers."

Janet exchanged a look with Laney.

"Chad, what was your grandfather's name?" Laney asked.

"Roger, but Dad said everyone called him Chip. He broke his front tooth trying to crack a walnut as a kid, and his parents couldn't afford to get it fixed. Dad's mom always told the walnut story to us grandkids in her thick East Coast accent, as a warning against trying to open things with our teeth."

Laney waited for Chad and Theresa to order then asked, "Chad, do you and Theresa have a few minutes to talk after you get your drinks? Maybe outside where it's quieter? I have something to share with you."

Janet said a quiet prayer for Laney as she got ready to tell Chad what they'd learned about Chip. Debbie served their coffees, and the Graysons followed the Farrells outside. Despite the sad news, Janet felt a wash of relief for Chad's family, who would at last have the answers they clearly craved. She sent a bittersweet glance over to Debbie.

Greg came to the counter and ordered a latte. "What's going on? You two got quiet all of a sudden."

Janet kept her voice low, even though Greg was the last in line. "Jonas Townsend fought alongside Chad's grandfather. His family never found out what happened to him. But Laney and Brian know. His body was mistaken for Jonas's."

Greg glanced in the direction of the window facing the platform. "Wow. God sure works in interesting ways."

Debbie filled the foaming pitcher with milk. "I wish the news was happier, but at least Chad will no longer wonder what happened to his grandpa."

Janet kept herself occupied behind the counter with Debbie and forced herself not to stare out the window. "He will also have the reassurance of knowing a friend was with Chip when he died."

When the café emptied, Janet went to the kitchen to wash utensils from the contest.

Debbie poked her head into the kitchen. "Janet, Laney, and Brian are getting ready to leave and want to say goodbye."

Janet wiped her hands on a towel. "Be right there." She took off her apron and walked out of the kitchen, approaching Laney with open arms. "I'm going to miss you."

"I'm going to miss you too." Laney wrapped Janet in a big hug. "But I'll be back. And I want to include you and Debbie when we set a date for dinner with Oskar."

Debbie reached out to hug Laney. "I'm guessing the Townsend house will be on the market soon. We'll be seeing a lot more of you if you buy it, and I couldn't be happier about that."

"Brian and I have been talking about that a lot over the past couple days. We're going to pass on the house. I'm going to email the Dennison Preservation Society on Monday to let Christine know we don't plan to bid on it."

"I hope Christine's reaction to your interest in the house didn't scare you away," Janet said. "She was truly remorseful the other day."

"It's not that at all. The more I thought about my grandfather and his full story, the more convinced I was that my grandfather would be all for a museum like the Dennison House. Especially considering its history as a boardinghouse for veterans."

"What about your B and B?"

"That plan hasn't changed, but there are other houses. Maybe we'll find one in Dennison. Or maybe someplace else. But wherever it is, I'm happy that our search led us here."

"Me too," Janet said. "Wherever you open it, be sure to let me know. Ian and I are overdue for a mini vacation."

Brian took his wife's hand. "We better hit the road, Laney. Janet, keep us up to date on the Dennison House. We want to be one of the first in line."

Janet watched the Farrells leave, waving. "I'm sad that we won't have Laney's themed B and B."

Debbie grabbed a towel and wiped down the counter. "But now we can go back to being prematurely excited about a museum that hasn't been purchased yet."

Janet shut the café door and flipped the sign to CLOSED. "And the next visitor who comes in with a story to shake up our little community."

Dear Reader,

When I was in the eighth grade, I set out to write my first book (other than the story about an orphan that I'd started on a doodle pad, complete with illustrations). It was a mystery, titled *The Letter in a Match Box*, typed single-spaced on both sides of the paper, using my parents' state-of-the-art IBM electric. I even designed my own cover. At the time, it was a crowning achievement, right up there with receiving the Home Economics Award.

I found my first "book" decades later and laughed so hard over the hokey dialogue and unrealistic plot that I could hardly breathe. Today, I remember that story with fondness and realize, *I should probably stop telling people I never expected to write mysteries. I wrote a practice mystery when I was thirteen.*

Since joining the Whistle Stop Café Mysteries team, I have discovered how fun it is to solve a mystery in a charming story world like Dennison, Ohio. It is exciting to help Janet, Debbie, and their friends—whether local or visiting—find answers, justice, or the missing piece of a historical puzzle one clue at a time.

I hope you enjoy reading *Rumors Are Flying* as much as I loved writing it. Thank you again to Guideposts and Susan Downs for inviting me to be part of your team, and for making the experience so much fun.

Happy Reading!
Jeanette

ABOUT the AUTHOR

Jeanette Hanscome is a multipublished author of both fiction and nonfiction, and a big fan of train travel.

When she isn't writing, Jeanette gravitates toward all things creative, especially now that her two sons are grown. After decades of singing without the ability to accompany herself, she took up ukulele during the pandemic with the help of YouTube videos. Experimenting with a variety of styles, including Celtic songs and music originally written for the lute (because why not?) is one of her favorite ways to relax after a day of writing. Jeanette writes and plays from her bedroom/office in the San Francisco Bay area.

A GLIMPSE of the PAST

These days, Americans try to cut back on sugar and fats as part of a weight-loss regimen or healthier eating plan. During World War II, all of America was put on a low-sugar, low-fat diet. Fighting in the Pacific impacted access to sugar and other goods, and the limited supply had to go to the miliary first.

In May 1942, Americans received their first ration books. As the war stretched on, rationing limited purchases of things like gasoline, tires, nylon, silk, and shoes, as well as foods such as meat, coffee, sugar, and dairy products. Though this was difficult, families saw rationing as their part in the war effort. Women learned to be creative in the kitchen, and cookbooks were packed with recipes that kept rationing in mind.

Instead of forcing those they loved to go without cookies, birthday cake, and other treats, bakers found tasty alternatives. They substituted butter with lard, shortening, or margarine. World War II-era cookbooks featured recipes sweetened with honey, syrup, or fruit and little or no sugar. Ingredients lists called for "fat" instead of specifying butter or lard, so bakers could use whatever they had on hand. Eggs were plentiful, so custards and low-sugar cakes and cookies showed up on tables often as well.

Some popular low-sugar baked goods included coffee cake, baked custard, apple pandowdy, and turnovers. People found a way to make ice cream with light cream and honey. Treats like soft molasses cookies were also much-loved, but because they called for a whole cup of sugar (a luxury in those days), families saved them for special occasions.

Now you have one more reason to be grateful for a full canister of sugar.

FROM the HOME-FRONT KITCHEN

Fruit Turnovers

This baked treat allows you to use any seasonal or canned fruit you have around, without any added sugar. Feel free to experiment with your favorite spices, add a drizzle of maple syrup or honey, sprinkle the turnovers with a blend of cinnamon and a small amount of sugar (after all, families did have some to use sparingly), or find something from your lunch to add like Julian did.

Ingredients:

About 2 cups of fruit, such as cooked apples, cherry pie filling, canned pears, or fresh berries

2 cups sifted flour

3 teaspoons baking powder

¾ teaspoon salt

1½ tablespoons of whatever fat you have on hand

Enough milk to make a soft dough (about ¾ cup)

Flour for rolling/cutting surface

Directions:

Preheat oven to 400 degrees.

Sift together dry ingredients in large mixing bowl.

Cut in fat thoroughly with pastry cutter or fork.

Add milk gradually and stir until soft dough forms.

Roll out dough on floured surface.

Cut dough into circles about 6 inches in diameter.

Spoon or place fruit on one side of the circle and fold empty half over fruit.

Crimp edges and place turnovers on lightly greased baking sheet or one lined with parchment paper.

Bake for 15 to 20 minutes or until golden brown.

Optional: If you happen to have some whipped cream or vanilla ice cream in your home-front kitchen, it will make the turnovers even more delicious.

Read on for a sneak peek of another exciting book
in the Whistle Stop Café Mysteries *series!*

HERE WE GO AGAIN

BY GABRIELLE MEYER

The aromas of burning leaf piles and the pumpkin spice latte she held in her hand filled the air as Debbie Albright walked toward Faith Community Church on Friday afternoon. October was one of her favorite months, not only because of the cooler temperatures, the colorful leaves, and all the pumpkin spice treats but because of her church's annual fall festival—which was only two weeks away. It was held on the last day of October and was the highlight of the month. Hundreds of adults and children attended from all over Dennison, Ohio, where they lived. Over the years, it had become a community outreach, and everyone looked forward to the event.

Debbie just wished there wasn't so much infighting on the event committee.

"If I hear Meagan Menard complain about the cost of sugar one more time," said Janet Shaw, Debbie's friend and business partner, "I will personally volunteer to make and donate all the caramel for the apples myself."

"She's complaining because she was put in charge of the food tent this year and would rather be helping with the games." Debbie took a sip of her latte and opened the church doors.

"She's complaining because she doesn't want to compromise," Janet said, and Debbie knew her friend was every bit as tired of the fighting as she was. "I wish they could all come together and find a way to work out their differences."

"The feud has been going on as long as I can remember. I doubt they'll figure it out this year."

"Don't you think it's strange that these women can get along all the rest of the year, but as soon as they start planning the fall festival, they suddenly can't tolerate each other?"

It boggled Debbie's mind as well, but she didn't have any answers. She and Janet had joined the committee to try to bring some healing to the group, but they hadn't made any progress—at least not yet.

The sound of raised voices echoed from the fellowship hall and into the front lobby as Debbie and Janet walked through the church. Debbie tried not to cringe as she finished her latte and tossed the to-go container in one of the garbage bins. Hopefully the drink would fortify her against the oncoming battle.

She'd been back in Dennison for over a year after living in Cleveland for most of her adult life. She and Janet had purchased the Whistle Stop Café in the old train depot and had spent the time since establishing their place in the community. Debbie had returned to her childhood church and thrown herself into volunteering wherever possible. She lived a rich, full life, and she had no regrets.

Yet when she heard Meagan Menard quarreling with Tammy Swenson, she started to rethink her choice to join this particular committee.

"Ladies, ladies." Pastor Nick Winston raised his hands to calm the group. "We won't get anywhere if we keep fighting. Surely there is a way to come together."

Debbie and Janet slipped into the room and took their seats at the large table in the corner of the fellowship hall. Six other women were already present. Two of them had their arms crossed and were glaring at each other with undisguised venom.

"I don't understand why we need to charge for the caramel apples," Tammy said. "This is a church. We shouldn't ask people to pay for food. It will limit the number of people we attract—people who don't usually come to church."

"And *I* say someone has to pay for them," Meagan insisted as adamant as Tammy. "We can't ask the congregation to hand over money every year for caramel apples, of all things."

"Churches don't exist to make money," Tammy protested. "We should offer this for free, out of the generosity of our hearts."

Several women nodded in agreement with Tammy while others sided with Meagan.

"Ah," Pastor Nick said when he saw that Debbie and Janet had arrived. "May I have a word with the two of you in my office, please?" The other women frowned as they watched Debbie and Janet stand, but at least they were quiet for the moment.

"We'll be back shortly," Pastor Nick said. "Tammy, will you please lead the meeting while we're away? We haven't yet decided if we're going to rent portable toilets or rely on the church's bathrooms. We're still having trouble with the plumbing."

Where is Edith? Debbie wondered. She was the board chairperson, and she usually led the meetings.

"If we charged more for the food and games," Meagan said, "perhaps we could afford to fix the plumbing."

Pastor Nick sighed as he motioned for Debbie and Janet to precede him out of the fellowship hall.

"I'm sorry things aren't going well," Debbie said to him.

"I try to prepare myself every year for this festival." He walked beside them toward his office. "But it gets harder and harder. I hate to see so much division and strife. I'm beginning to think it's not worth it."

"At least they don't carry it over to the rest of the year," Janet said.

"For now," Pastor Nick said, "but I fear that may soon change. It's one of the reasons I want to speak to you. I'm sensing a deepening level of hostility, and it's not good for anyone."

He opened his office door and flipped on the light then closed the door behind them while Debbie and Janet took a seat. He sat across from them, his face weary as he folded his hands on the desk. "I'm afraid I received some bad news today."

Debbie frowned and leaned forward. "What's wrong?"

"Edith's husband called and told me that she fell last night and is in the hospital with a broken hip."

"What will happen with the festival?" Janet asked.

"I'm afraid we only have two options," Pastor Nick said. "We can either appoint a new chair, or we can cancel the event—perhaps permanently."

Debbie thought about all the families who enjoyed the festival, viewing it as an alternative to the scarier Halloween activities the community offered. Her own childhood memories of the event brought her warmth and joy. They couldn't cancel or stop it completely.

"What do you suggest?" Debbie asked.

"I was hoping that the two of you could step in and cochair the event this year."

Debbie bit her lip. She and Janet were busy with the Whistle Stop Café, and she was hoping to get a few projects done at her house before winter. She had purchased it when she moved to Dennison, but the old home still needed some updates. Did she have the time to take over a large festival—one that was only two weeks away?

Janet's frown revealed her own concerns. Being part of the committee was far different from taking it over completely. It was a big responsibility.

"We can't do this without a chairperson," Pastor Nick said. "Unfortunately, all the other women are too opinionated about the event to lead without bias. You two are the most levelheaded committee members we have, and you've shown your strength in leadership in so many ways. We could really use your help."

"I'm not sure I can take on such a big commitment," Janet said.

Debbie started to shake her head as well, but she couldn't stop thinking about the children who eagerly anticipated the event each year. Not only those in their church but also in the larger community.

"It would only be for two weeks," Pastor Nick said. "We need someone who can make the rest of the decisions going forward and steer the others in the right direction." He leaned forward, his kind blue eyes bright. "What I'm hoping is that you can show the others how to work together for a common purpose. I hope we can bring healing to this committee and to the event. It's a lot to ask, but if anyone can do it, it would be the two of you."

Debbie couldn't deny that his words were flattering, but could she and Janet bring the committee together? It was a lot to ask, especially since the group had been at each other's throats for years.

"Take some time to pray about it and talk it over between you," Pastor Nick said. "I'll need an answer by tomorrow. The elders have been concerned about this committee for a long time, and I have a feeling that when they hear about Edith, they'll recommend that we cancel the festival if we don't have another chair. It would be a shame."

"We can't let them cancel it," Debbie protested. She didn't need time to think about it. If the alternative was losing the festival, she would chair the committee alone if she had to. "I can do it."

"I was going to say the same thing," Janet said. "It'll be a lot of work, but we can't let it go. I'd hate to disappoint the kids."

Pastor Nick's face lit up. "You'll cochair the event?"

"Absolutely," Debbie replied.

"Of course. I don't think Ian will mind," Janet agreed. Ian was Janet's husband and her biggest supporter. As far as Debbie knew, he rarely minded when Janet volunteered or got involved in the church or community. As the chief of police in Dennison, Ian understood the church's importance to the town.

"Wonderful," Pastor Nick said. "I'll let the elders know that you have agreed to take over. They'll be so pleased."

"I hope the other committee members will agree with them," Janet said. "After all, Debbie and I are the newest members of the group. They might not take too kindly to us telling them what to do."

"We won't tell them what to do," Debbie said. "We'll gently suggest the direction the committee should take and hope they don't push back."

Janet lifted her eyebrows in a silent implication that Debbie was being too optimistic.

"Come on," Pastor Nick said. "Let's go let the others know."

Debbie stood and followed the pastor and Janet back to the fellowship hall.

Her stomach was in knots as they reentered the room.

The other women raised their heads expectantly as Debbie and Janet took a seat.

"Is there something we need to know, Pastor?" Tammy asked.

"Unfortunately," Pastor Nick said, "Edith had a fall and will be out of commission with a broken hip for several months. I've asked Debbie and Janet to cochair the event in her stead."

For a second the others stared at them in surprise—and then the room erupted in a cacophony of objections.

Debbie's head was pounding when she and Janet pulled away from the church an hour later. Neither spoke as Debbie drove down the road.

The silence was a treat after what they had endured. The committee members had voiced their loud concerns about Debbie and

Janet taking over, and they had fought to be heard, pushing their own agendas and opinions.

"Could you stop by the café on your way back to my house?" Janet asked. "I forgot my cell phone."

"Sure," Debbie said.

"What have we gotten ourselves into?" Janet asked, echoing Debbie's thoughts. "I'm afraid we're in over our heads. Those women are even more combative than before. Will any of them respect us as cochairs?"

"If we can't find a way to bring the group together, the elders will cancel the event for sure," Debbie said. "It would solve everyone's problems."

"But it would be sad to see the event end. Tiffany counted down the days to it every year as a little girl."

"I did too," Debbie said. "And Greg said it's his boys' favorite church event as well. We can't give the elders a reason to cancel it."

"Then we need to get the group on the same page."

"I don't understand why the caramel apples are such a big deal," Debbie said. "Do you think they're so petty that it's actually about the apples? Or do you think there's something deeper going on?"

"I don't know," Janet said. "But you and I need to decide how we want the festival to proceed this year and then stand as a united front when we tell them."

"Agreed." Debbie parked at the depot and shut off the car.

The Dennison Depot was a centerpiece in the community. During the war years, it had served as a Salvation Army canteen and an important stop for service personnel leaving their homes and loved ones behind to fight in the war. Some had dubbed it Dreamsville, USA, for the warmth and hospitality that had been given to them by the canteen workers. A museum filled most of the depot with the Whistle Stop Café in the other part.

Museum curator Kim Smith stood near the front desk when the two friends entered the depot.

"Just the people I wanted to see," she said. "I didn't think I could wait until tomorrow morning to tell you."

Debbie smiled as they approached Kim. "What can't you wait to tell us?"

"Mark found something interesting in my office when he was replacing an outlet today."

Mark Thomas was an electrician and a general handyman who did odd jobs around the depot.

"Something good or bad?" Janet asked.

"Good. I think." Kim frowned. "I guess it could be bad though. I hadn't thought about it like that." She motioned to her office. "It's on my desk."

The museum was quiet, which meant there probably weren't any visitors. That made sense, as it was close to closing time.

Kim opened the door to her office, which had served as the station-master's office before the building was turned into a museum. Kim's mom, Eileen Palmer, had been the depot stationmaster throughout World War II and had used the very office and desk that Kim still used. Now, Eileen lived at the Good Shepherd Retirement Center, where Debbie and Janet visited her often.

"What is it?" Debbie asked as she entered the office.

"This." Kim held up a yellowed envelope with the letters *USO* on the front. "It's full of money!" she said. "More than five hundred dollars, and all the bills are dated from the 1940s or earlier."

Debbie took the envelope and opened it to find the money tucked neatly inside. She frowned as she handed it to Janet.

"Where did Mark find it?" Debbie asked.

"In the wall—behind that panel." Kim pointed to the wall where a wood panel had been removed and was propped up next to the opening. "It was at the bottom, so if the panel had been off for work in the past, it would have been easy to overlook. Mark had to drill a hole in the bottom of the wall, and that's how he found the envelope. There was a rubber band around it, but when we tried to take it off, it fell apart."

"Why does it say USO?" Janet asked.

"I'm not sure. It could stand for United Service Organizations, a nonprofit that helps active service members transition to civilian life. They've been around a long time. But I can't say for sure. I don't know anything about it, except what I told you," Kim said as she took the envelope back.

"What will you do with it?" Debbie asked.

"First, I'll call the police to see what they think I should do. I just want to make sure it's not stolen money. I'll decide from there what to do with it."

"Maybe your mom remembers what it's about," Janet suggested. "If anyone knows, it would be her."

As the depot stationmaster, Eileen had seen a lot of events over the years. If five hundred dollars had gone missing, she would know about it.

"That's a good idea," Kim said. "I was planning to run out to see her this evening. Would you two like to come with me?"

Debbie brightened. "I'd love to hear what she has to say about it. And I haven't had a good visit with her and Ray for a while."

Ray Zink was a longtime resident of Dennison and the person who had owned Debbie's house before her. She had purchased the house from Ray right before he moved into the same retirement center as Eileen. Both were a wealth of knowledge about Dennison, especially the depot and the war years.

"Mom's told me there were several USO events at the depot over the years," Kim said, "but I don't remember her ever telling me about losing five hundred dollars."

"Maybe the USO on the front of the envelope doesn't have anything to do with the events that took place here," Debbie suggested. "Maybe it was just being reused."

"Or the USO stands for something else," Janet said. "Maybe it's someone's initials."

"That could be," Kim said. "Five hundred dollars was a lot of money during the war. Someone had to be aware of the loss."

"Or someone put it there for safekeeping and forgot about it." Debbie shrugged.

"I suppose there are a lot of possibilities," Kim said.

Debbie pulled out her cell phone and found an online inflation calculator. She held it up and said, "Five hundred dollars in 1945 was worth more than eight thousand dollars in buying power today. That was a significant amount of money during the war years. Someone must have noticed it went missing."

"But why was it in the wall?" Kim asked. "Who would put it there? I hope my mom has some answers."

"I'll call Ian," Janet said. "He should be off work soon, but maybe he can stop by and let us know what he thinks about the money." She stuck her hand in her pocket then said sheepishly, "I forgot why we stopped by. I left my phone in the kitchen. I'll be right back."

Debbie suppressed a laugh as Janet left the museum and unlocked the door to the café.

They had made several improvements to the café over the past year. The restaurant was the reason Debbie had returned to Dennison after leaving her corporate job in Cleveland. She had needed a slower pace and had convinced her lifelong friend, Janet, to open it with her.

Not only had the café filled that need, but living in Dennison had proved to be more exciting than Debbie had bargained for. She and Janet, with the help of several friends, had solved several mysteries, both old and new.

Would the origins of the money be another mystery to solve? Or would Eileen know exactly why it was hidden in the wall?

Debbie couldn't wait to find out.

A NOTE FROM the EDITORS

We hope you enjoyed another exciting volume in the Whistle Stop Café Mysteries series, published by Guideposts. For over seventy-five years, Guideposts, a nonprofit organization, has been driven by a vision of a world filled with hope. We aspire to be the voice of a trusted friend, a friend who makes you feel more hopeful and connected.

By making a purchase from Guideposts, you join our community in touching millions of lives, inspiring them to believe that all things are possible through faith, hope, and prayer. Your continued support allows us to provide uplifting resources to those in need. Whether through our communities, websites, apps, or publications, we inspire our audiences, bring them together, and comfort, uplift, entertain, and guide them. Visit us at guideposts.org to learn more.

We would love to hear from you. Write us at Guideposts, P.O. Box 5815, Harlan, Iowa 51593 or call us at (800) 932-2145. Did you love *Rumors Are Flying*? Leave a review for this product on guideposts.org/shop. Your feedback helps others in our community find relevant products.

Find inspiration, find faith, find Guideposts.

Shop our best sellers and favorites at
guideposts.org/shop

Or scan the QR code to go directly to our Shop

Find more inspiring stories in these best-loved Guideposts fiction series!

Mysteries of Lancaster County

Follow the Classen sisters as they unravel clues and uncover hidden secrets in Mysteries of Lancaster County. As you get to know these women and their friends, you'll see how God brings each of them together for a fresh start in life.

Secrets of Wayfarers Inn

Retired schoolteachers find themselves owners of an old warehouse-turned-inn that is filled with hidden passages, buried secrets, and stunning surprises that will set them on a course to puzzling mysteries from the Underground Railroad.

Tearoom Mysteries Series

Mix one stately Victorian home, a charming lakeside town in Maine, and two adventurous cousins with a passion for tea and hospitality. Add a large scoop of intriguing mystery, and sprinkle generously with faith, family, and friends, and you have the recipe for *Tearoom Mysteries*.

Ordinary Women of the Bible

Richly imagined stories—based on facts from the Bible—have all the plot twists and suspense of a great mystery, while bringing you fascinating insights on what it was like to be a woman living in the ancient world.

To learn more about these books, visit Guideposts.org/Shop